HAUNTED LAFAYETTE, LOUISIANA

CHERÉ DASTUGUE COEN

Haunted America

Published by Haunted America
A Division of The History Press
Charleston, SC 29403
www.historypress.net

Front cover: Courtesy of Joshua Coen.
All internal photos courtesy of the author.

First published 2013

Manufactured in the United States

ISBN 978.1.60949.746.0

Library of Congress CIP data applied for.

CONTENTS

Introduction

For years I was a ghost writer.

Not the person hired to write a book by another, but one who loves to relate a captivating ghost story. Even in my youth I couldn't resist a tale of a haunted house, a strange occurrence, unexplained phenomena—even UFOs. The paranormal fascinates me.

Perhaps it's my journalism background, because not many among our curiosity-driven industry can resist a tantalizing story. Maybe I just wanted a glimpse into the unknown or to incite a chilling reaction from my reading audience. But more importantly, I needed to know why ghosts of the living still haunt a place. I wondered why some appear to hang around homes and buildings while others supposedly roam the countryside and linger in cemeteries. Some claim souls attach themselves to furniture, allowing antique lovers to bring home more than they bargained for. And if people find themselves trapped on this earthly plane, I wondered if it was possible to lead them on to a better place.

After years of writing ghost stories for numerous publications—not to mention the endless paranormal shows I watched on TV—I found myself more frustrated than ever in discovering who these people are who are haunting South Louisiana, why they are still here and whether we can help them cross over. So many times I've interviewed homeowners discussing their ethereal specters, and most of the time they are happy to have such unusual guests in their homes, as if they have become part of the family. It makes one wonder if ghosts remain on this plane, perhaps, to aid us in some way. The myriad questions plague me.

The other elusive element of ghost hunting is capturing an apparition with my own eyes. I've had dozens of unexplained experiences, but like TV's TAPS (the Atlantic Paranormal Society), I've worked hard to "debunk" these moments. Because at the end of the day, an unusual noise in an old house could very well be the house "settling," kids forgetting to turn out a light or shut a door or a cat crawling up a window screen in the middle of the night hoping someone will let it in.

And yet some things can't be explained.

I used to catch movement in my peripheral vision in our first home shared with my husband and two sons in Baton Rouge when I was a features writer and editor at the *Advocate* newspaper. A ranch house built in the 1970s, the home wasn't settling, nor did it own decades of fascinating history. But every now and then, I could swear someone moved in the kitchen, like a sudden blur across my line of sight. When I turned the corner, however, no one was ever there.

One day, an author friend came to visit, a woman sensitive to other spiritual planes. She slept in our guest bedroom on the other side of the house, a cozy room where I wrote my novels across a hallway from the kids' bedroom. When she joined us for breakfast the next morning, she blurted out, "You know, you have a ghost in this house."

While she described a petite, elderly woman who appeared by her bed the night before, my husband and I exchanged nervous looks. My first thought wasn't to question the sanity of my friend but whether I would admit to seeing what might have been paranormal activity in the kitchen.

Instead, my husband beat me to it. Turns out we'd been witnessing the same phenomena—blurs through the kitchen area as if someone had walked through—but had both chalked those moments up to our imaginations. Bruce had even seen what had looked like the outline of a woman.

"She's definitely here," my friend had said. "She wants you to know that she's watching over the kids."

My husband was and still is convinced the apparition was his mother, who had recently passed when this incident occurred. When I had asked my next-door neighbor about the elderly lady who had owned the home before us, she told me the former owner had passed away inside the house.

Bruce and I never fully captured the apparition apparently watching over our children—whoever she was—but we were happy for her company and wished her well.

When my family and I moved to Lafayette in yet another postmodern ranch-style home, we couldn't image any ghosts inhabiting our suburban property. The only sounds we heard at night were our pets demanding to go in, then out, then in again; the bullfrogs in the coulee out back (that's a ditch for you non-Cajun readers); and the birds at sunrise outside our bedroom window.

Our younger son, Taylor, who was a young teen at the time, had a different experience. He encountered clunking noises in his bedroom ceiling and the feeling that someone had walked up to his bed and stood over him. He swore a teenage girl walked past him down the hallway one night. "The computer screen also flashed and the lamp flickered just a few seconds before and there was a rushing of wind sound when the girl appeared," he later told me. When he had followed to investigate, no one was there.

All of this occurred during our fascination with *Ghost Hunters* on TV, so I tried to find rational answers to the mysteries. I didn't want Taylor to think I didn't believe him, but on the flip side, I couldn't ignore that the TV show might have set off his already vibrant imagination.

Then came two more sensitive friends.

I met Allyson Glynn Schram when she hosted metaphysical classes at South Louisiana Community College in Lafayette. I was invited to discuss my latest book on gris gris bags and show class participants how to make their own version of the magical items. Because Allyson receives messages from spirits, she will be having a normal conversation with you one minute and channeling a message the next. She pulled in an ancestor of mine during a phone conversation once, a man she described as a Lincoln lookalike who had something to do with horses, whom I recognized because of the name she received. I knew of the man, not what he looked like, of course, but that he was a native of France and an early Louisiana census taker and justice of the peace. Because she instigated me thinking of him, I googled his name on a lark. I found an obscure reference to him judging horse thieves in court, something I never knew about before our conversation.

Schram does psychic readings, and curious to see what else she could obtain from "Spirit," which is the term she uses for those in another plane communicating with her, I drove to her home in Arnaudville to receive one. One of the many messages she had for me was a vision of a ball of light not far off the ground, traveling through my house. It flowed freely, heading out into the backyard and returning to roam through the house, Schram had said. I had no idea what this meant—my newly deceased dog perhaps—but I began to wonder if my new home had a few balls of energy we couldn't see.

Next came my coauthor on the gris gris book, Jude Bradley, a California medium and cleanser of homes. She spent the night in Taylor's room while Taylor took to the couch and, like my previous experience in Baton Rouge, had something interesting to report at breakfast. She witnessed a young girl in Taylor's room sitting by the window singing a French song while playing with dolls. This pleased Taylor to no end, who exclaimed, "I told you there was something going on in my room!"

Once both my sons passed puberty and grew into men, however, the unusual activities in the house ceased. I couldn't help but wonder if the ghosts had been more fascinated with their hormonal energies and left when the chaos diminished. On the other hand, since the disappearance of one of our cats, there's been a strange noise in the brick floor of the living room at night, usually happening well after dark and sounding as if a heavy foot is walking on the floor. One theory is that it's our sweet kitty coming back to visit from another plane of existence. Another is that it's a loose brick that pops when the temperature beneath it changes. More than likely, it is the latter, but we all can't help but wonder when the brick sounds in the dog days of summer (no pet pun intended).

And then there was that heavy sigh one night at my shoulder while I watched TV on the couch.

Like so many people I interview, I've never been afraid of those who have passed on, unless they were mean people who carried that negativity into death. I still long to know who they are and why they are still here, and I hope to catch a clear image. In the stories that follow I attempted to find as much information as possible to identify the ghosts lurking in Lafayette, Louisiana, and the surrounding region. I enlisted the help of local libraries, historians and genealogy sites to put names to ghostly faces and learn of their stories. Some were too elusive to find, although I hope that readers with inside information may provide answers to the mysteries after enjoying this book (and write me if they do!). Some mysteries behind the region's ghost stories were solved—or at least their stories are now being told.

As for the questions surrounding ghosts in general, I am no closer to the answers than I was at the beginning of my career, although my "sensitive" friends validate what I believe to be real and true.

The questions of who the ghosts are and why they are here I will leave to you, dear reader.

CHAPTER 1

THE GHOSTS OF CAFÉ VERMILIONVILLE

Lafayette, Louisiana, touts itself as authentically Cajun and Creole, home to world-famous Cajun and zydeco music and the most delectable cuisine on earth. People come to Lafayette to "pass a good time," two-step at historic dance halls, fish or paddle the lush wetlands, enjoy world-renown festivals and soak up the unique culture.

And some people don't want to leave.

It's hard to pinpoint who may be haunting the buildings and countryside of Lafayette and the surrounding region. Native Americans hunted the prairies and wetlands for centuries until the French arrived, who claimed the vast territory of Louisiana for King Louis XIV. For a while, Spain occupied the colony during the time of the Acadian expulsion from the Canadian Maritimes, and Lafayette and much of South Louisiana soon became the new home for these displaced "Cajuns." African slaves worked the region's plantations, and some either bought or were rewarded with their freedom, creating the largest group of free people of color in the United States at one time in neighboring Opelousas. Other nationalities followed, too—Germans, Irish and Sicilians, to name a few.

There's a reason residents call Lafayette the "Hub City." The town sits nestled in the southwestern prairie of Louisiana, like the hub of a wagon wheel with spokes reaching out in all directions. There's the Atchafalaya Basin to the east, the historic Opelousas District to the north, rice country to the west and the sleepy bayous and Gulf Coast to the south.

Lafayette was originally called Vermilionville and consisted of a collection of residences and businesses hugging the slow-moving brown waters of Bayou

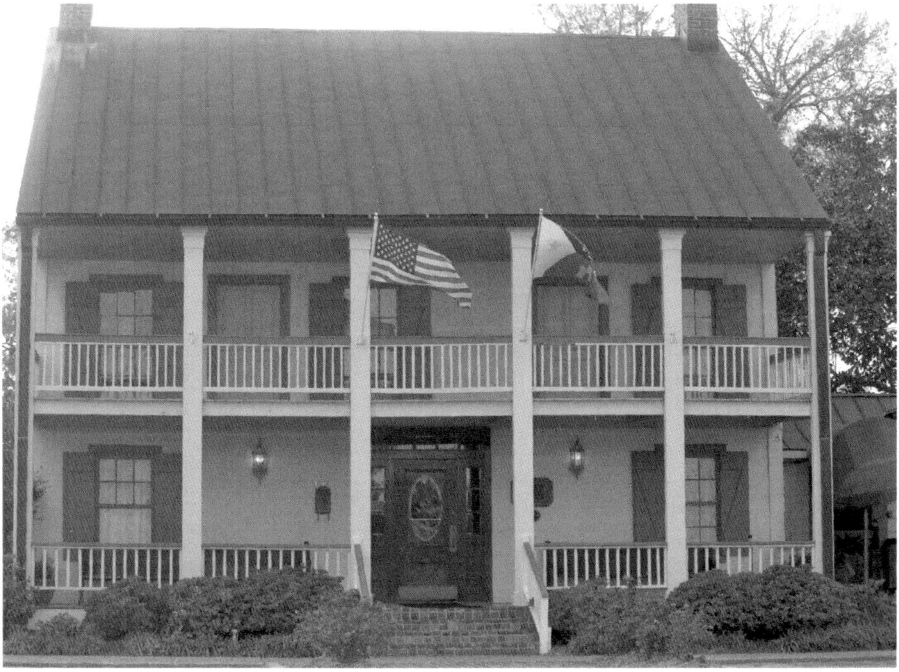

Café Vermilionville is one of the oldest structures in Lafayette and includes at least one ghost.

Vermilion. In 1821, prominent landowner Jean Mouton donated land for a church, one that would be named for his patron saint, St. John's Cathedral. About the same time, the Catholic Church created a parish for the region extending from Mouton's plantation to the Gulf of Mexico and west to the Sabine River, Louisiana's border with what was to become Texas. This new parish was named for the American Revolutionary hero, the Marquis de Lafayette. In 1884, when the town's charter was revised, both the town and the parish had become known as "Lafayette."

One of the oldest buildings in Lafayette, dating back prior to 1818, has evolved from Lafayette's first inn into an elegant restaurant serving fine Cajun and Creole cuisine. Café Vermilionville sits back from busy Pinhook Road, a reminder of a quieter, simpler time, and offers customers a respite from the harried world. The two-story building contains both Anglo-American and French features with dual chimneys at each end and double porches on each floor. It was first used as an inn for travelers moving up and down Pinhook Road (earlier the Old Spanish Trail) and crossing the nearby Pinhook Bridge over Bayou Vermilion, about two miles south of the center of present-day downtown Lafayette and Mouton's St. John's Cathedral.

During the Civil War the building was unfortunately in the wrong place.

Major General Richard Taylor and his Confederate forces had retreated to Lafayette with Union major general Nathaniel P. Banks hot on his heels. When Taylor reached Bayou Vermilion on April 17, 1863, he crossed over and promptly burned the Pinhook Bridge. Banks arrived soon after and began firing at the Confederates over the water, and the Rebels returned the fight with artillery. The duel continued until dark fell, and the Rebels retreated to Opelousas.

In the middle of the skirmish was the building that is now Café Vermilionville.

Once the fight was over, Banks and his Union soldiers rebuilt a bridge over Bayou Vermilion on April 18 and took over the building. At the time, Henry (Hans) Louis Monnier lived in the home, a Swiss native who had no interest in the war. Story has it that when Banks rebuilt the bridge and made it to the other side, he spared the home in honor of Monnier's neutrality.

Later that year on October 9, 1863, a more intense battle occurred at the bayou, not too far from the old inn, this time involving the home of former Louisiana governor Alexandre Mouton and other members of his family.

At which time the occupying Yankees insulted a Frenchman's wife at the Swedish man's inn is not clear, but the tale lives on through the decades.

"The rumor is that one of the Yankee officers paid too much attention to a local woman and the husband killed him," said owner Ken Veron Sr.

In the lobby of Café Vermilionville, in the left hand corner, is a spot where the Yankee soldier reportedly was murdered. The restaurant's floors were replaced in the 1950s—although what exists today still offers that same historic home feel. The original flooring, however, contained bloodstains where the Union soldier had fallen.

And that's not all that's lingering at Café Vermilionville. Two customers have witnessed a man in the bar with a handlebar mustache—both described the same man. A bartender also watched as several liquor bottles slid off a shelf, as if an invisible hand had pushed them.

"He quit," Veron said of the bartender. "Three or four bottles just fell off the shelf."

Another time when a freeze hit the area, Veron arrived early on a Sunday morning to check on the pipes, which can easily break because of their exposure. He checked the restaurant for breakage and then headed back to the lobby area. When he entered the room, it was unusually cold—and not because of the cold snap.

"I felt so strange," Veron said. "I turned and went."

Veron's son, Ken "Poncho" Veron Jr., also came in during a chilly Sunday to check on things and heard a "ssh" underneath a table. He, too, left quickly.

Poncho Veron had worked as a funeral home ambulance driver in high school and college, actually living in the funeral home while attending college, but he had never felt so frightened, he said.

Most of the unusual activity occurs with electrical appliances or computers, the Verons say. For instance, the old cash register used to have a key to turn it on and off. At the end of the day, the Verons would put a key in the register and then move it to Z to start the compiling of the day's receipts and to initiate a printout.

"We were having drinks one night and the cash register starting running and Z-ing out," Veron said.

When they came to investigate, there was no key in the cash register.

The strangest experiences happened when they renovated the restaurant.

"There was a whole bunch of little things," Veron said of the paranormal occurrences, "but the strangest was when we did alterations."

One day the fire department arrived to inspect the building's renovation. They requested that the Verons build a subfloor between the first and second floors since the ancient house had a simple floor that served as both second room floor and first floor ceiling. Code dictated that the Verons block off the upstairs so that customers would keep off a floor deemed unsafe for crowds. So Ken boarded up the two second-floor rooms, closing the doors with plywood.

One of the rooms that were sealed up contained a desk next to a wall sporting an oversized historic map of Louisiana. The other walls contained several old paintings with brown paper on the back.

After the rooms were boarded up, the restaurant was plagued with electrical problems, and computers continually crashed. There were even sparks flying from an electrical line that electricians said went nowhere.

Later, Poncho Veron and two friends opened up the second-floor room. When he first pulled the plywood free and entered, he was greeted with a blast of air that felt as if the pressure had dropped significantly. But the scene before them scared them even more. The giant map had been ripped off the wall and lay in tatters on the floor. The other paintings were also lying on the floor, the brown paper on the backs ripped as well. The scene appeared as if a petulant child had had a tantrum.

Once the doors to the upstairs rooms were opened and remained clear, the electrical problems ended, and the computers worked without fail. That is, until I arrived to discuss their ghosts for this book. Not too long after I interviewed the Verons, I ran into Poncho's wife, Andrea Veron, who informed me that they had experienced mechanical problems immediately after I left.

Another time, a couple enjoying a meal downstairs witnessed candles being pushed off a shelf by invisible hands. They thought it was weird but kept eating, thinking maybe they had imagined the event. The same thing happened fifteen minutes later. When they discussed the phenomenon with the waiter, and learned of the house's possible ethereal residents, the couple asked to visit the upstairs rooms, where they caught orbs on their camera. When they asked the waiter if a presence was hanging around the upstairs rooms, they heard a large, unexplained boom.

Who Remains at the Inn?

Whatever or whoever is causing these electrical anomalies and moving things about, it might be the young daughter of Dr. Percy M. Girard and his wife, Leila Beatrice Singleton. The building was the couple's country home around the turn of the twentieth century while Dr. Girard practiced medicine out of his downtown Lafayette home at 1122 Lafayette Street, once the home of Louisiana governor Alexander Mouton (ironically the Civil War neighbor of the Swedish owner of the Pinhook property) and which now houses the Lafayette Museum.

Dr. Percy, as he was known, was a well-liked physician in Acadiana, and he helped establish the Carrell-Girard Clinic for disabled children in Dallas, Texas. At his Pinhook country home in Lafayette, he grew sugar cane and cotton.

Dr. Percy's daughter Mary Gladys Girard was born on November 21, 1905, the youngest of Dr. Girard's five children. Just shy of her seventh birthday, she contracted, it was believed, scarlet fever. The story goes that Dr. Percy traveled to New Orleans to retrieve a doctor or medicine but young Mary Gladys perished before his return. She died November 26, 1912, and is buried in the Lafayette Protestant Cemetery a few blocks down Pinhook Road.

Many people believe one of the lingering energies of Café Vermilionville is Mary Gladys. A manager once saw a little girl sitting in a wing-backed chair in the lobby wearing a blue dress and swimming in a blue aura. Some people have seen a little girl staring out onto the world from the upstairs window. In the 1950s Horace Rickey owned the building, and he once asked the Verons if they had seen any ghosts.

"They [the Rickeys] indicated it was a little girl," Veron said.

For the most part, Mary Gladys's antics are playful. For instance, servers put four pats of butter on plates every night. When the servers turn around to do other duties and turn back, they will sometimes find three pats of butter remaining. Poncho Veron once moved the same roll of paper towels five times from a spot before realizing that something was up.

When Louisiana Spirits visited the restaurant to investigate, their evidence was minimal except for a few flashlight experiences. But they searched census records and are pretty confident the ghost is that of Mary Gladys.

"Based on the census records it follows what people have experienced," said Jennifer Broussard of Louisiana Spirits.

After Mary Gladys's death, Dr. Percy's health deteriorated, and he retired from practicing medicine. Dr. Percy died December 11, 1944, at the age of eighty-five of kidney failure at his Lafayette Street home. He, too, is buried at the Lafayette Protestant Cemetery.

I failed to witness anything unusual at the restaurant—which serves up delicious Creole dishes and an outstanding bread pudding by the way—but my son Taylor accompanied me for the interview and on several occasions was convinced someone was tugging on his shirttail, as if a small child was trying to get his attention.

CHAPTER 2
LITTLE BROTHER'S BED-AND-BREAKFAST

The following story, "T'Frere's Bed & Breakfast: Where Maugie, Pat and a ghost named Amélie provide an award-winning overnight experience," was originally published in Country Roads *magazine of Baton Rouge in October 2011.*

Some say that the personalities of ghosts in the afterlife are much like the ones they had while living. Amélie Comeaux who haunts T-Frere's Bed and Breakfast in Lafayette was a "canaille," a mischievous girl, and her antics in death reflect this wily nature.

"She's typically Cajun," said Maugie Pastor, who owns the bed and breakfast with her husband, Pat, and runs the business with the help of her sons, all of whom have experienced Amélie's presence.

Amélie Comeaux married young in the late nineteenth century, and became pregnant. She lost the child and soon afterwards lost her young husband. Amélie moved in with her brother, Oneziphore Comeaux, known as "T-frere" or little brother. At his house in Lafayette, she mourned her family. Later, she found work as a math teacher to area youth.

At thirty-two, Amelie caught a fever and stumbled to the backyard well for water late one night and mysteriously fell in. Because the Catholic Church labeled it a suicide, she was not buried on sacred ground.

"Amélie doesn't like change," Pastor said, noting that the majority of Amélie's hauntings came within months after they had purchased and moved into the bed and breakfast. She would hear banging and things breaking in the kitchen—only to find nothing out of place. A visitor claimed to have had his toes pulled in the night.

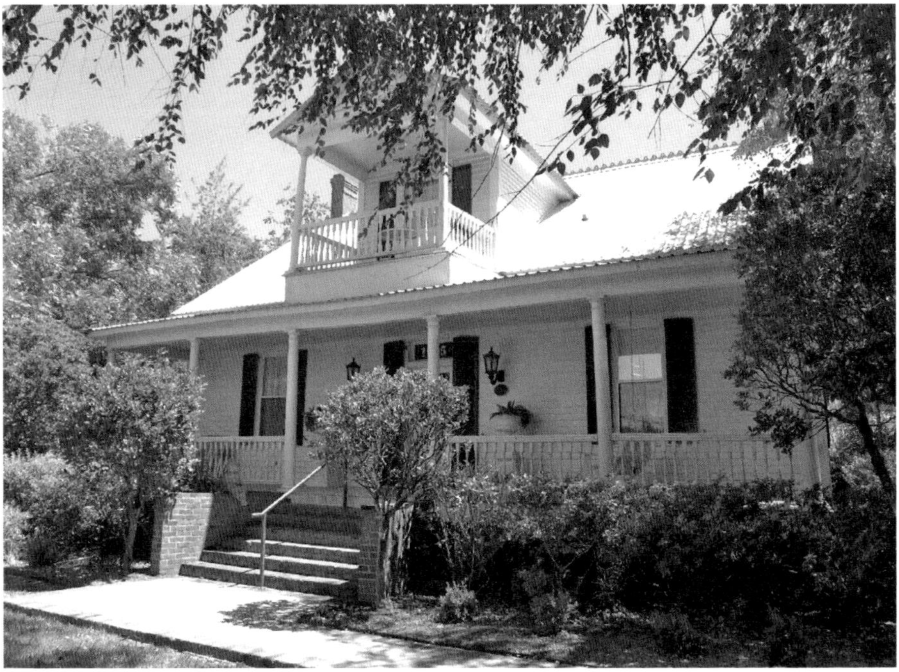

A petite French woman by the name of Amélie still lives at T-Frere's Bed and Breakfast in Lafayette.

The most unusual experience happened to her son, Jeremiah, when they were moving in. Maugie told him to bring everything he needed to the new house because they weren't making any more trips that night. Jeremiah forgot his math homework and was stressing on how to tell his mother when the math paper suddenly appeared.

"I heard him come bounding down the stairs," Pastor recalled. "He said the paper that he needed floated down from the ceiling."

Family members searched the room but couldn't find a logical explanation, chalking it up to the petite math teacher who remained in the house.

Today the bed and breakfast offers four bedrooms in the main house and two guest rooms in the Garçonnière out back, but only the main house has paranormal experiences, Pastor said.

Maugie and Pat Pastor, former Lafayette restaurateurs, cook up gourmet breakfasts every morning and after-dinner drinks and Cajun canapés on the gallery in the afternoons. Maugie creates eight different types of "Oooh La La Breakfasts" for her guests, including cheese cake stuffed pancakes, crawfish enchiladas and bread pudding, to name a few.

"If you stay longer than eight days, I put you on a diet," she said with a laugh.

Because visitors staying at T-Frere's would always ask numerous questions about Cajun culture and history, the Pastors' sons have started a side business offering boat cruises on the Vermilion River, appropriately called "Pastor Brothers Cajun Excursions." The brothers give lessons in crawfish peeling and Cajun dancing and side trips to Vermilionville and the Jean Lafitte National Historic Park and Preserve.

"We give them the greatest Cajun experience of their lives," son John said.

Although most come to T-Frere's for Lafayette's great food and culture—many not knowing about its haunted history—some do visit to catch a glimpse of Amélie. Guests have reported sightings and unusual happenings, such as the Texas family who spotted a woman standing by the arbor when they returned to the house after dinner. The woman spoke to the mother in French, which she relayed to Maugie Pastor the next morning.

"She repeated what she [the spirit] had said and I asked her how she knew French since she was from Texas," Pastor explained. "The woman replied that she was originally from Breaux Bridge. How did Amélie know she was from Breaux Bridge?"

Others who have seen the apparition described Amélie as petite, speaking only French and wearing her hair back in a bun. An elderly couple staying in the Leah Room lost their car keys, and John Pastor puts the blame on *canaille* Amélie.

"We tore the room apart," he recalled. "Their keys were between the mattress and the box springs. These people were in their eighties so there is no way they could have lifted that mattress."

"I believe there is no such thing as death," said Arnaudville medium Allyson Glynn Schram when asked for her thoughts about Amélie. "The physical body gives out, which is what we call 'death,' but our spirit, our soul is eternal."

Schram is the author of the eBook series *The Medium and the Mortician*; she's married to South Louisiana mortician Charles Schram.

She believes geography plays more of a role in hauntings or spirit contact than family. For instance, Amélie haunts T'Frere's because it was her home.

"There are repeated imprints in the land of those who go on ahead," Schram explained.

The well that Amelie drowned in that fateful night has been filled in, but the T'Frere's backyard continues to settle around it. In fact, the Pastors had to reinforce the house in the exact spot where the well once stood.

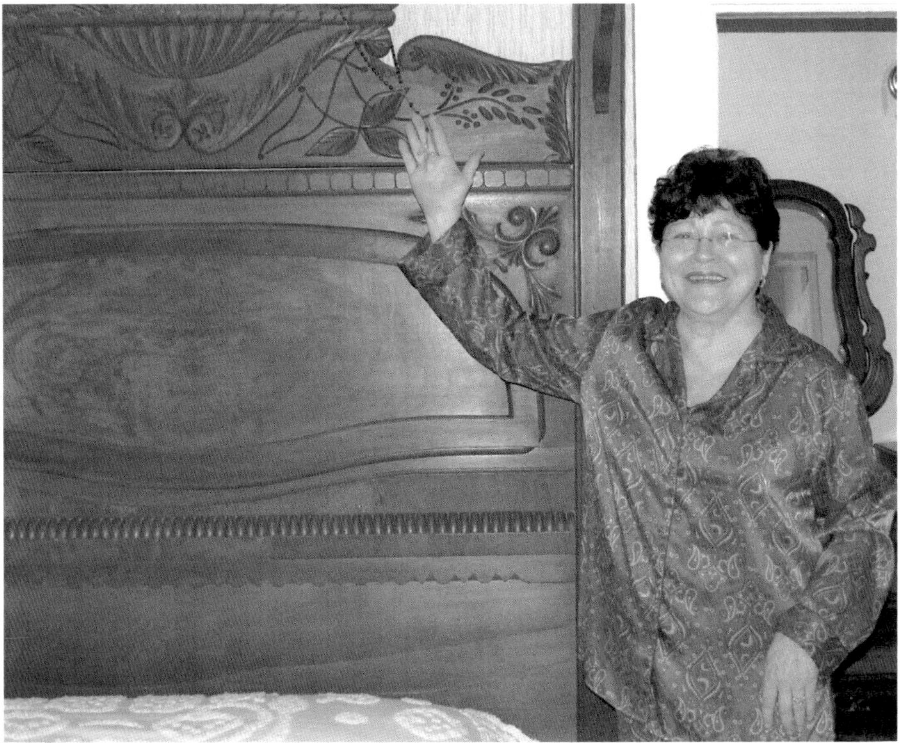

T-Frere's owner, Maugie Pastor, displays one of her crucifixes over a bed at T-Frere's Bed and Breakfast in Lafayette. Pastor isn't afraid of her ghost, who she believes is a kind French woman.

NOTE: Since writing that article I found some interesting information about the house at the corner of Verot School Road and Eraste Smith Road. The property on which the house sits was bought by Oneziphore Comeaux, known as "T-Frere" or "Little Brother," in 1886. Comeaux built the house in the 1890s. The two-story structure was home to Oneziphore Comeaux until his death in 1916, but his descendants remained there until 1952. Oneziphore's wife, Aurelia Broussard Comeaux, died in 1950.

After Aurelia's death, the house and land was then purchased by Kossuth Willis Benoit, followed by Blair Smith, Dan Ritchey, Lewis Donlon, Pierre D. Olivier Jr., artist Will Hinds, Dr. Kenneth Purcell, Mr. and Mrs. Charles Moseley and finally the Pastors.

According to *If They Could Talk: Acadiana's Building and Their Biographies* by Mario Mamalakis, both Peggy Moseley and Mrs. Olivier experienced paranormal activity in the house, both stating that it was of a nonthreatening nature. On one occasion, Mrs. Mosely saw someone running her fingers across her piano keys, even watched the keys depress, but no one was there. Items on the pantry shelf would routinely fall off, much like Maugie Pastor described. Olivier's bottle collection on a shelf above the sink was swept off and onto the floor as well, missing the sink completely, which would have made more sense if it had been a natural occurrence. Mrs. Olivier also reported female laughter in the front room, sounds like glass breaking in the attic and other unusual, unaccountable noises. Both Olivier and her mother saw a loaf of bread rise off a table without help from a living hand and then fall to the floor.

"Mrs. Moseley says that both she and Mrs. Olivier are convinced that there is a 'Presence' in the house but that it is a benign one and tends to make the house even more interesting," Mamalakis writes.

Is the ghost haunting T'Frere's Bed and Breakfast really Amélie, the petite French math teacher? According to *Haunted Hotels*, Moseley's neighbors are the ones who relayed the story of the young Cajun woman.

"One of the Moseley's [*sic*] neighbors identified Amélie as an unhappy woman who had died in the house in an accident at the age of thirty-two," according to *Haunted Hotels*. "Moseley's mother saw Amélie in the garden, describing her as 'a little Cajun lady, wearing her hair in a bun, dressed in a gown of ashes-of-roses color, with a cleft chin. She spoke French.'"

Like Pastor's son, Amélie helped the Moseley children with their math problems.

CHAPTER 3

CAUCHEMARS IN THE DORMS

THE GHOSTS OF THE UNIVERSITY OF LOUISIANA AT LAFAYETTE

It was like something from your average teenage Hollywood scary movie. Three college students were hanging out in a dorm room at three in the morning and discovered more than they bargained for.

It all began with a news article of the June 24, 1973, tragic fire of the UpStairs Lounge in New Orleans. Ask South Louisiana residents today about the French Quarter event, and it's a vague memory, even though thirty-two people died that night at the corner of Chartres and Iberville Streets. Today, the UpStairs Lounge fire is considered New Orleans's deadliest arson attack and the worst attack on LGBT people in U.S. history.

About sixty people of the Metropolitan Community Church, an international Protestant denomination that supports gay rights, were gathering in the lounge on Sunday, June 24, 1973. The lounge had once been a temporary home to the church, and it still attracted members. That night, the group included the Reverend Bill Larson. Those hanging out at the UpStairs Lounge on June 24 had just come from the final day of Gay Pride Weekend in New Orleans—a quieter event because the gay community back then kept mostly underground—and were listening to pianist David Stuart Gary performing "United We Stand" by the Brotherhood of Man and joining in on the song.

When the buzzer rang from the doorway downstairs, it was assumed that someone had called a cab. Luther Boggs, a teacher, descended the wooden steps to the first floor down the building's only staircase. When Boggs opened the front door, a fire breathed in the stairwell's oxygen and erupted, charging

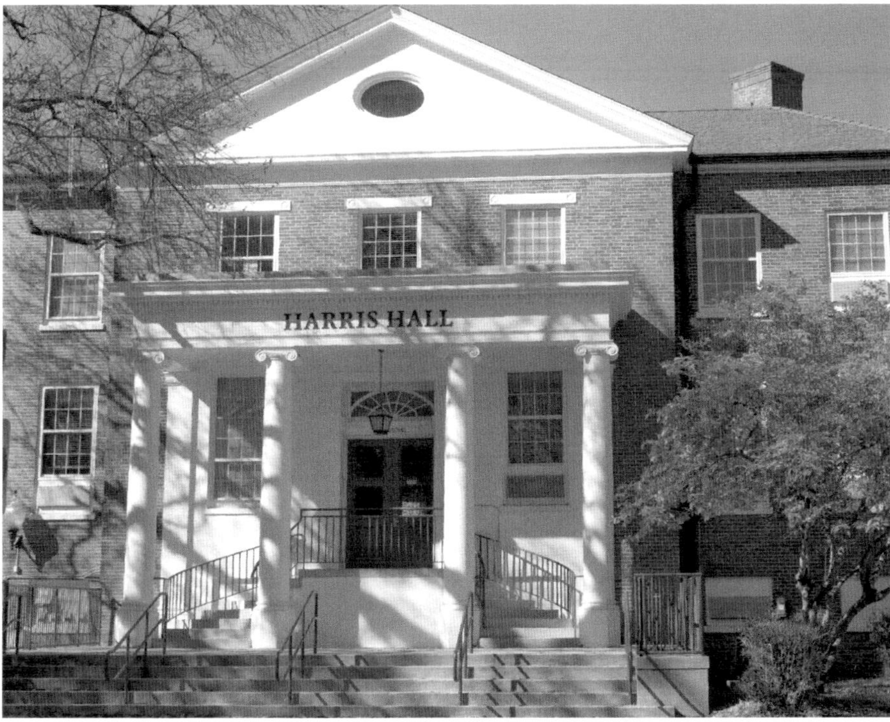

Harris Hall is one of the dorms at the University of Louisiana at Lafayette that's supposedly haunted.

up to the second floor like a deadly fast-moving train and blocking the front way out of the bar.

The fire department was alerted at 7:56 p.m., and bartender Buddy Rasmussen led some of the bar's inhabitants through a back door to safety. Others were not as lucky. Those trapped within the second floor attempted to flee through windows but were deterred by window bars. One man managed to make it through the barred window only to die from the fall. Reverend Larson died cornered at one window, his charred remains trapped halfway through the bars. Metropolitan Community Church assistant pastor Duane George "Mitch" Mitchell, who had managed to escape to safety, died when he returned to free his partner Louis Broussard. Their remains were found clinging to one another. George Matyi also escaped to safety but returned to help others, his body later found embracing two other victims.

The fire lasted a mere sixteen minutes, but the damage was extreme. Twenty-nine people died within its flames with three others later perishing from their wounds. Fifteen more people were injured. Among the dead were Mitchell, Boggs, Gary and Mrs. Willie Inez Warren and her two sons, Eddie Hosea Warren and James Curtis Warren.

It was believed that earlier that day Rogder Dale Nunez had been thrown out of the bar, making him the prime suspect. Nunez had a history of mental problems. Police questioned him, but his mental instability raised its head. He was taken to Charity Hospital, where he slipped their bonds and escaped. He was never apprehended but, soon after, killed himself. Witnesses have claimed he bragged about starting the fire, pouring Ronsonol on the staircase and lighting a match.

The fire was tragic enough, the worst fire-related incident in the city's history up to 1974, including the massive French Quarter fire of 1788 that nearly burned the entire city. But the lack of public outcry or empathy was equally heartbreaking. The grisly scene of Reverend Larson trapped in the window bars was published by the Associated Press in newspapers, and police took their time removing his body. The overall coverage either failed to mention a gay church in a gay bar or used heartless language to describe the scene. Even quotes from bystanders using anti-gay language were included in the stories.

Because the victims were mostly gay men, there was only a small prayer service by the Reverend William P. Richardson of St. George's Episcopal Church, who was later reprimanded for his actions. The Unitarian Church and St. Mark's United Methodist Church eventually held memorial services on July 1.

Three of the victims' bodies were never identified. Some believe they were buried with victim Ferris LeBlanc at Holt Cemetery, also the final resting place of musicians Charles "Buddy" Bolden, Jessie Hill and Jewell "Babe" Stovall.

University of Louisiana at Lafayette freshman Chase Lubag learned about the fire after viewing an exhibit on the tragedy at the New Orleans Contemporary Arts Center. He decided to research the event, even visiting the bar site in the French Quarter, now known as the Jimani Lounge. After reading newspaper accounts of how the thirty-two people had died and the injustices that followed because they were gay, including cruel jokes, he became angry.

"I was charged," Lubag said. "I was enraged."

The owners of Jimani Lounge claim the place is haunted and enlisted the help of the Atlantic Paranormal Society (TAPS) for an episode of TV's *Ghost Hunters* (Episode 15, Season 8). TAPS investigated the lounge and discovered paranormal activity, such as unaccountable voices and unusual sounds on their recorders and spiking meters when the arsonist was mentioned. They also visited Holt Cemetery, where the four victims are reportedly buried, and the mortuary next door in Mid-City New Orleans.

Did one of these apparitions follow Lubag home to his dorm room in Lafayette? At first he saw a genderless face in his dorm room window at Coronna Hall, a dark sunken image "like black sand," Lubag described it. Then came the knocking on the window at night, when the closest tree branch was at least ten feet away.

"The air was always heavy," Chase described his dorm room, although he felt the spirit was more attached to him than trying to do harm. "Whatever it was, it was always very protective of me."

Coronna Hall is actually a spanking new building built over the previous dormitory, which was built in 1957, and named for B.N. Coronna, a supporter of the university. His daughter was one of the school's first graduates. The original building was recently torn down and a new building—made to appear like its previous incarnation—took its place. Outside Coronna and neighboring buildings is a long, lovely row of live oak trees. Dorm residents are treated to views of the trees' ample arms stretching out, the resurrection ferns that expand in rain and retreat on dry days and haunting Spanish moss that drips from the lush tree branches.

Around three o'clock on an early November morning, Lubag invited my son Taylor and a friend to his third-floor dorm room in Coronna. On this particular visit, their friend felt uneasy and depressed, the first time he felt so upon entering Chase's room.

While standing in the room's corner, Taylor saw a glowing blue light along the threshold of the room's door.

"And then suddenly it was gone," Taylor said. "It was like someone was flashing a light under the door."

At the same time someone grabbed him from behind, like someone had jumped him, wrapping his or her arms around his shoulders and holding on, he said. Only no one was there.

Taylor freaked, stood and yanked off his jacket. Suddenly, the tightness disappeared.

"It felt like someone was on my back, grabbing me from behind," he said. "It felt like a piggy back."

Flustered from Taylor's experience and the appearance of the blue light, the threesome moved to the dorm hallway and decided to meditate on what had just happened. Taylor closed his eyes and felt himself falling into a deep meditation.

That was when he saw her—she was wearing a similar jacket as the one he had just removed.

"I saw a woman in that jacket being burned alive by a man who was in all red," Taylor said. "He was by the dorm closet with the air conditioner. Then a man came into the room and muttered words over a book, and the man in red got sealed in the closet."

Taylor describes the man with the book as wearing a brown fedora, brown jacket, black pants and a gray shirt and tie.

At this point, the three students didn't know what to make of what had just happened, so they moved down the hall to the third-floor student community room where they imagined they would be safe. Even with the bright lights, comfy chairs and warm carpeting, curiosity followed them there, and they began using Lubag's iPhone recorder in the hopes of capturing a live voice. They asked numerous times if the spirits were still there, but no one answered, until finally a faint woman's voice whispered in a sing-song style, "Still here."

At one point, Lubag said, "Say something if you wish to be known."

Taylor answered, "What happened?"

And then a voice belonging to neither of the men uttered, "Nothing."

An exasperated sigh clearly not belonging to any of the students can be heard during one of the conversations, and when Lubag asks if the spirits were visiting from the UpStairs Lounge, a thump is heard.

During the time of the taping none of the students had heard these remarks; it wasn't until later when they played back the recordings that they realized not all of the comments had belonged to them.

But they certainly felt the presence.

Lubag felt cold energy while being continually touched on the knee and the shoulder. "It was literally on me," he said.

Lubag has since cleansed his dorm room with salt and burning sage and left prayers of protection about, even though he doesn't believe the spirit or spirits are there to harm him. He never cleansed the air conditioning closet, however, because that closet has always been locked.

As for the UpStairs Lounge history, the Metropolitan Community Church held a twenty-fifth-anniversary service in 1998 and placed a commemorative marker in front of the Jimani Lounge, the scene of the infamous fire. No one was ever charged for the crime.

URBAN MYTH OR CAUCHEMAR?

Coeds plunging to their deaths or taking their lives are common legends in colleges around the country. I wasn't surprised to find two among the dormitories of the University of Louisiana at Lafayette, once known at different times in history as the Southwestern Louisiana Institute and the University of Southwestern Louisiana.

I've heard that a girl was killed in the 1960s when she entered an out-of-service elevator that slipped and decapitated her. The girl remains on the campus, living between worlds, and helps live female students find lost items. People have claimed to have seen a woman with a '60s hairstyle waving from dorm room windows.

"James" on the website GhostsofAmerica.com wrote:

> *I was walking on the USL* [University of Southwestern Louisiana, now University of Louisiana at Lafayette] *campus one evening in 1980 just passing in front of Denbo Dorm on the way to the Student Union. As I looked up at the dorm I saw a foggy image of a college girl with a sixties haircut style looking at me. She was smiling and as I was about to wave she vanished, the blinds behind her did not move. She just vanished. I walked a little faster. The next day in math class I was speaking to a classmate about it and she said all the people in the dorm know about her. She is the ghost of a girl who died from a fall down the elevator shaft back in the 1960s. She said the students like her and that she looks out for them.*

Denbo Hall was built in 1968 and named in honor of writer Anna Margaret Denbo, who fought for a parish tax in the late 1890s to fund the first public school in Lafayette. Denbo was the author of two novels, *A Romance of Old New Orleans* and *Sunshine and Shadows*, and she once lived next door to Dr. Percy M. Girard in downtown Lafayette (see chapter 1). The original dorm has since been torn down, but a new building named in honor of Denbo now exists within Legacy Park, an apartment-style housing building on the campus.

When I mentioned the legends of dorm apparitions to Lubag, his eyes lit up. He's heard the elevator story too, although in his version the girl fell down the elevator shaft and haunts Harris Hall, an old dormitory near his that was built in 1939 and named for former state superintendent for education Thomas H. Harris. The ghost of Harris Hall—which still stands today—is of the Casper variety, he said, helping the girls who live there.

In a 2012 article by the school's newspaper, the *Vermilion*, author Jessica Manafi reports the girl's name as Lily and concurs the accident as happening within an "out-of-commission elevator" in Harris Hall.

"As story has it," the article attests, "the elevator fell on her and decapitated her. Since the incident, the elevator has been sealed and closed off behind a steel door."

There's another story, this one centering on Baker-Huger Hall but concerning another closed-off room. This legend tells of a female student who committed suicide in one of the rooms at the original Baker dormitory, built in 1950 and named for Elizabeth Fowles Baker who was matron of the girls' dorm and one of the university's first faculty members. The student who moved into the dorm room where the girl took her life also committed suicide—exactly one year, to the day, later. Because of the incidents, and to break what might have been an evil spell, the administration bricked up the room.

Both Baker and Huger Halls have since been torn down (Huger was also built in 1950) and replaced by lovely new dormitories, but students find the new Baker quite eerie. And they don't always know the old legends.

Baker resident Ariella Robinson complained of the dorm being haunted, for instance, but of what she had no idea.

"So I was at the dorm, and I would hear what sounded like someone clawing at the wall in my suitemate's bathroom," Robinson related to my son Taylor when he mentioned I was doing a book on possible university paranormal activity. "Then I would open the door and no one would be in there or outside the bathroom. And it would continue for days. Then I called a CA [Community Assistant] to come look at possible water damage on my ceiling in my room. The CA thinks I am crazy. He says it is just the pipes. I don't think so. Then on top of that the watermark on my ceiling looks like someone was walking on my ceiling, more like standing upside down on my ceiling."

One night she heard a strange tapping at her window.

"Right now I am currently trying to find out if the tapping outside my window is someone's cruel joke or something else," she said.

As for Taylor's experience, the creature on his back could have been a "cauchemar."

In French, *cauchemar* means nightmare, but in Cajun Country, it could refer to a spirit that torments people by riding on their chests or backs. If you examine the word, *cauche* is derived from the Old French verb *cache*, *cauchier*, meaning "to press," and from the Middle Dutch *mare*, meaning "phantom or nightmare." *Mar* even has Proto-Indo-European origins meaning "malicious female spirit."

In a 1985 article in the *Morning Advocate* of Baton Rouge, the late folklorist Dr. Patricia Rickles of Southwestern Louisiana University (now University of Louisiana at Lafayette), described *cauchemar* as "a nightmare spirit that chokes and suffocates people in their beds." Rickles claimed that numerous people she had interviewed over the years believed in them, including one who felt its presence in the university dorms.

"Lately, there was a student on campus who left school and went home because he said there was a cauchemar in the dorm," Rickles is quoted as saying in the article. "And he wasn't staying somewhere there was a cauchemar."

CHAPTER 4
LONGTIME DOWNTOWN RESIDENTS

While writing a ghost story for the *Advocate* of Baton Rouge in 1995, I interviewed Connie Gaitlin, a friend of Maugie Pastor of T-Frere's Bed and Breakfast (see chapter 2). Gaitlin assisted Pastor with occasional ghost tours and was no stranger to the paranormal. One night when giving a tour at T-Frere's Bed and Breakfast, she counted her guests, and everyone was accounted for. And that's when she heard the upstairs door open and close.

But Gaitlin had a better story to recount when I called her in 1995. She worked at Cathedral Carmel School in downtown Lafayette, a Catholic school affiliated with the Sisters of Our Lady of Mount Carmel and the De La Salle Christian Brothers and established in 1846. The current buildings date back to 1919.

One Halloween, she photographed kindergarteners in their costumes on Alford professional film and found more than she bargained for when the photos were developed. A "huge" figure in black boots, a clerical collar and a tattered robe was standing behind the kids.

Confused, she mailed the photos to the Ilford Company in England to see if they could explain the anomaly.

"They told me they didn't know what it was," Gaitlin told me during her interview. "But the image was made with light."

One theory is that the man was a former brother who lived at Cathedral Carmel. There had always been rumors of a one-legged brother haunting the gym, making the lights go on and off, and people claimed to have heard

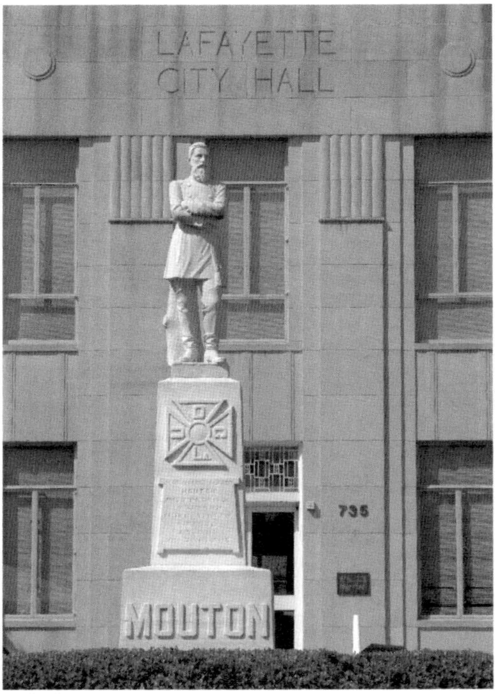

Downtown Lafayette, founded by Jean Mouton on Mouton's vast property, has its share of ghosts. Civil War hero Alexandre Mouton, grandson to Jean, is shown here in front of the old city hall.

sounds of a leg scraping across the gym's floor—only one leg, of course.

When I worked at the *Advocate* in Baton Rouge, I routinely visited Lafayette to cover events. I used the bureau office on Johnston Street in downtown Lafayette—an old two-story house surrounded by graceful trees and a long driveway to the street—to file stories back to Baton Rouge.

Bureau reporters used to recount tales of unusual sounds emanating from the old home. One staff member, who was the first to arrive at work one morning, found the building empty. When she entered one of the building's ground-floor offices, the phone lit up with an intercom call ringing from her own phone upstairs. Another time staff members witnessed a woman dressed in Civil War–era attire standing at the top of the rear stairway.

When the *Advocate* sold the property and moved to a more modern building about two blocks away, the home was relocated. Today, only the vacant lot remains. One has to wonder whether the lady preferred the comfort of the live oak trees on Johnston Street or if she left with the house.

CHAPTER 5
"GATEWAY TO THE WEST"

SCOTT'S BEGNAUD HOUSE

Becca Begnaud is a *traiteur*, or Cajun faith healer, who lives in Scott, a town only minutes from Lafayette. Scott is known for its boudin, or Cajun rice sausage, and for being nicknamed the "Gateway to the West" when the railroad came through at the beginning of the twentieth century. When Begnaud was hired to be the director of La Maison de Begnaud, Scott's Heritage and Interpretive Center, we laughed at the coincidence.

Her new job includes programming community events such as Cajun jam sessions, cultural talks, French tables where Cajun French speakers can enjoy conservation in their native languages and more.

"And by the way," she said, "there are ghosts in the house."

Begnaud works as a traditional Cajun traiteur, as well as being a Reiki Master and Healing Touch Practitioner. Her grandfather was a traiteur, too. The practice is a form of healing that involves prayers passed down verbally through the generations and considered sacred. People would visit traiteurs—and still do—to cure themselves of warts, skin rashes, sunstroke, headaches, toothaches and the like. Money was never exchanged, but the healed would be free to donate to the church to thank God for the cure or leave tokens of their appreciation to the healer. Begnaud has even written about her experiences in *Louisiana Folklore Miscellany* in an article titled "Life of a Healer."

The healing arts don't necessarily mean viewing the dead, Begnaud is quick to point out; she's never viewed a ghost in her life, but she believes ghosts exist. Odd sounds at night occurred at her family home in the country,

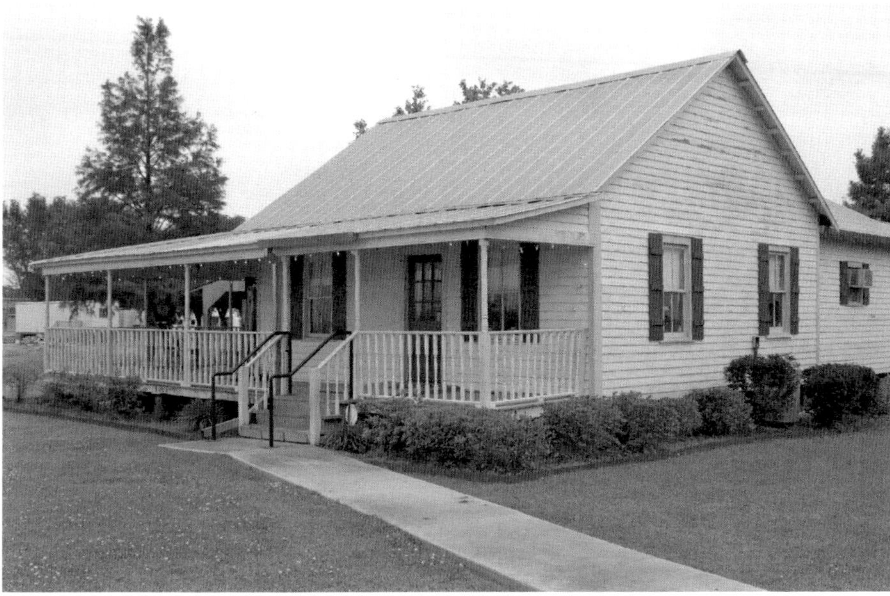

The Begnaud House in Scott serves as the city's welcome and tourist center. It's also home to three ghosts.

like someone walking through hallways when no one was there. Becca's sister was insistent the ghost was their grandfather.

"My sense was my grandpa was walking through the house," Begnaud said. "But why? I couldn't imagine what would keep a man here."

Begnaud wondered if her grandfather were hanging around to make sure Becca's mother was okay. Or perhaps he had died too suddenly from his brain aneurysm and failed to realize he was dead. Begnaud asked a psychic friend if she could help her grandfather cross over to the spiritual plane. They held hands and spoke to the grandfather in French, explaining that all family members were in good hands in the living world and that it was time to go.

"No one has seen or heard from him since," she said. "I don't have a way of verifying, but I feel that."

When Begnaud insisted there were ghosts at the Begnaud House-Scott Welcome Center, I expected more stories, but she continued to insist she's never actually seen one.

Donna Thibodeaux, however, has seen more than her share.

Thibodeaux works daily at the Begnaud House and was warned upon her hiring that weird things happen from time to time. The cash register, for instance, may be working fine all day and then suddenly go blank while still being on. The computer does the same, even though it's clearly plugged in. For a while, the coffee pot would go on and off and on and off.

"It was like someone was standing there, hitting it off and on," Thibodeaux explained of the coffee pot. And when they were just about to buy a new one, the weird motions ceased.

Another day, the doorbell rang, as it does when people enter the house, and Thibodeaux would get up to greet customers. Only every time, no one would be standing in the foyer. This went on for hours.

"At the end of the day, we were very tired," she said.

Thibodeaux believes the Begnaud House residents are three people who have passed: a woman who loves to disrupt the electrical appliances, a man who prefers the rocking chairs on the porch and a child who enjoys throwing the DVDs off the shelf and waiting at the door, gazing out on the world. She's seen all three in some form or another but not clearly enough as to make out their features.

"They're hazy but you can tell they're there," she explained. "It's not a scary feeling. This must have been their home at one time."

Thibodeaux senses they are related to the house but perhaps not of the same generations. On occasion, they speak to their companions, sometimes asking the child to stop pushing all the DVDs onto the floor.

"It's aggravating when the electricity goes out," she said. "But I hope they stay."

The Begnaud Family

Just who haunts the Begnaud House? The Acadian home was donated to the City of Scott for its use as a tourist information center by the descendants of the Joseph Begnaud family. The home originally existed north of Interstate 10 and was moved to its present location by Scott's walking trails and arboretum, only five hundred yards south of the Interstate 10 Exit 97. It's a perfect location for a tourist center, offering maps and brochures, a small library with books on the city's history and a souvenir and gift shop with books, CDs and DVDs on Cajun and Creole culture plus local handcrafted items and Louisiana products.

On several walls are historic photos of Scott, including a portrait of Cidalise Ophelia Boudreaux Begnaud, who once lived in the house. Cidalise was born April 7, 1859, in Lafayette, the daughter of Zephrin Boudreaux and Celestine Delhomme. She married Joseph Begnaud, the son of Alexandre Begnaud and Eliza Constantin, on December 15, 1879, in Lafayette, her second marriage.

The home had been given to Joseph and Cidalise Begnaud as their "matrimonial domicile" according to an article in the *Great Scott Herald* newspaper. After the birth of their children—Noemi Celestine Begnaud, Joseph Alexandre Begnaud and Jean-Zepherin Begnaud—the family of five lived in the home until the fateful day of February 8, 1893, when Joseph Begnaud killed himself.

The *Times-Picayune* newspaper of New Orleans reported:

> *Prominent Man's Suicide*
> *Mr. Joseph Begnaud of Lafayette, Takes His Own Life in a Fit of Temporary Insanity.*
>
> *Lafayette, La., Feb. 8—(Special)—The suicide of Mr. Joseph Begnaud today caused much surprise and sorrow to his many friends throughout the parish. The unfortunate man was a resident of the First ward and lived near Scott. He leaves a wife and three children to mourn his untimely end.*
>
> *The rash deed was committed during a temporary period of insanity, by means of a shotgun, which the victim used by placing the muzzle in his mouth and discharging the contents into his head. Mr. Begnaud was an esteemed citizen, and at the time of his death was a member of the parish school board, representing the First ward.*

Perhaps it's Joseph Begnaud enjoying the warm South Louisiana climate on the rocking porch.

"Most Atrocious Crime"

Or perhaps the ghost haunting the Begnaud House is Martin Begnaud, Joseph's younger brother, born November 24, 1850, who never married. Martin operated a grocery and dry goods store in Scott and kept valuables in a backroom safe. Joseph and Martin's brother, Simeon Begnaud, ran a saloon next door to Martin's grocery.

On the evening of April 22, 1896, Martin Begnaud was approached at the store by Alexis and Ernest Blanc, two young Frenchmen working on the neighboring plantation of Drozin Boudreaux. The two brothers had argued with Martin and then apparently convinced him to open the safe. After stealing the money, they gagged Martin and tied him to his bed, where they proceeded to stab him fifty-two times in the neck and chest with a makeshift dirk created from a three-cornered file. The men even plunged the dagger in Begnaud after his death, according to newspaper accounts.

Begnaud's servant found the horrific scene at 7:00 a.m. the following morning and alerted the authorities.

"Mr. Begnaud was dead when found, his hands and feet were bound together, and he was lying on the bed in a pool of blood, his body had been literally perforated with stab wounds, 52 having been counted," reported the *Lafayette Advertiser* of April 25, 1896. "The safe door was open, and its valuables missing. It is supposed that robbers secured about $7000 in money. He was tied with a bandana over his mouth and around his head (calico) and his hands were bound behind his back, feet secured too with strong ropes… he was then completely wound up, head and all, in a sheet of white domestic and thrown upon the bed."

The emerging details were gruesome and shocked a nation as the story was told far and wide.

Robbers "began their work of torture, by dealing him short stabs with some triangular shaped dagger, 52 in all, forming a complete necklace of wounds beginning on the side of the neck and passing down over the chest and up to the neck again on the opposite side, thus forming a complete chain; then the final stab was given over the region of the heart piercing this organ through and through, and was sent with such violent force that it left the point of the dagger's hilt upon the mouth of the wound."

After the Blanc brothers killed Martin, they buried the money and the instrument of crime and waited a few days before leaving Scott. They then spent months touring France, Mexico and the United States, spending every last dime of Martin's money. When all was spent, the not-too-bright Blanc men returned to Scott, asking for their old jobs back at the plantation. Drozin Boudreaux alerted the sheriff, who arrested the two, who promptly confessed everything.

A funeral for Martin Begnaud was held April 24, 1896, at the St. John Catholic Church in Lafayette, which "was packed to its utmost capacity by a sympathizing community," wrote the *Lafayette Advertiser* of May 2, 1896. "Father Forge took the opportunity to address the people on the subject of

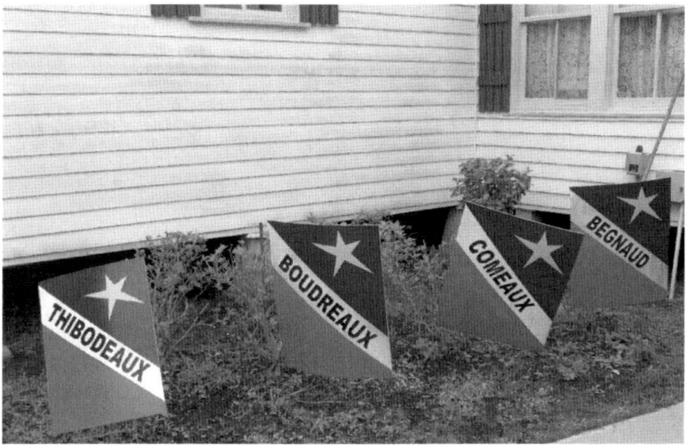

Scott's Heritage and Interpretive Center, in the Begnaud House, serves as a center for Cajun culture.

the crime and administer the consolation of religion, as well as to impress wise counsel as to the duty of good citizens."

As Father Forge remarked on the crowds gathered to show affection to Martin Begnaud, he admonished the murderers for the "most atrocious crime in the annals of this parish…"

When Father Forge added, "Here lies before us the inanimate body of him you loved so well, stricken down in the prime of manhood by the fatal blow of midnight assassins," the audience "melted to tears," the article stated. At times, Father Forge himself became so overcome with emotion he couldn't speak.

Even more popular was the neck craning to watch Alexis and Ernest Blanc first get tried and then convicted in court. Charles Alexander Homer Mouton and descendant to the founder of Lafayette defended the duo, but since they had confessed to their dastardly deeds, the jury spent little time handing over a conviction, sentencing the brothers to death by hanging. The latter was well attended as well.

Visitors walk daily through the doors of La Maison de Begnaud, Scott's welcome center, and participate in the Cajun music jams and cultural events. Families with children visit the neighboring pond to feed the ducks or visit the antique train car that honors Scott's railroad history. Little do they realize the tragedies that befell the Begnaud family at the turn of the twentieth century or the ghosts who cling to its memories.

Thibodeaux doesn't believe that the female ghost of the Begnaud House is Cidalise. And since Joseph and Cidalise's three children grew to adulthood, the child specter is the greatest mystery of all. Perhaps she's just a lonely soul finding solace at the weekly jam sessions and watching the visitors come and go.

CHAPTER 6

LOUISIANA SPIRITS

ACADIANA'S GHOST HUNTERS

Jennifer Broussard always had an interest in ghost hunting but really made an effort to learn more about paranormal investigating three years ago.

"It was initially just to get over my fears," she said.

She joined Louisiana Spirits, a paranormal investigative organization with chapters throughout the state. Each of the five chapters—southwest, southeast, south central, north and central Louisiana—offers a professional investigation of properties that are reportedly haunted.

"We seek out the historic locations, but a lot of the private residences seek us out," Broussard explained.

Louisiana Spirits also offers instruction at the University of Louisiana at Lafayette Continuing Education, a leisure class broken up into three sessions. Students first learn ghost hunting techniques and how to use equipment, and then they investigate a property at night. During the last class, students analyze the evidence they received during the investigation.

On regular investigations by the organization, they might do additional research into the hauntings, said investigator Charles Gardner, who joined Louisiana Spirits after taking the class. He once heard "Caroline" spoken at a home in West Lake, near Lake Charles. He later researched the property and found that a Caroline once lived there. After that, he was hooked.

The South Central group of Louisiana Spirits has investigated many properties in Lafayette and surrounding areas. Sometimes investigators pick up EVPs (electronic voice phenomena) or witness spikes in their EMF (electro-magnetic fields) meters or K-2 meters, devices that measure magnetic fields. At times, Louisiana Spirits members fail to pick up anything paranormal, even though stories abound on the property's hauntings.

"You can't make ghosts participate," Broussard said. "It just means they weren't ready to play."

For instance, at the Steamboat Restaurant in Washington, about forty-five minutes north of Lafayette, Broussard and company experienced paranormal activity on the first visit and none on the second. On their first visit, as they were sitting by the bar, they heard noises in the kitchen and were convinced a live person was in the room with them.

"We thought someone was in the building because we heard someone come right at us," Broussard explained. "It was so real we took the tire iron off the wall. Something was coming right at us."

The video they took shows what looks like a shadow of a person walking across the dining room with an elbow coming into frame. They aired the video on Louisiana Spirits TV across the Acadiana Open Channel, and the screening drew about three hundred people, Broussard said.

At the Steamboat Restaurant, the group also caught someone whistling loud and then someone singing in a jazzy voice, "It's so cold in here."

Paranormal evidence ranges from voices caught on tape or video to anomalies captured in photos, such as unusual lights, mists, smoke and shadows. EMF meters can spike without warning and temperatures may suddenly drop. At the Egan Hotel in Crowley, group members asked the spirits to make the temperature drop, and it fell several degrees. At the Abbey Players theater in Abbeville, Louisiana Spirits found a traveling cold spot in the dressing room and were treated to the sound of someone not living saying, "Hi," when investigators were in a room greeting one another.

In some cases, equipment fails.

"They do pull energy, from batteries to people," explained Gardner. "On several occasion we've had batteries die…and activity happens."

On the flip side, "orbs" of light captured on film and video can easily be bugs, dust or moisture in the humid South Louisiana air, Broussard said. Ectoplasm could be moisture, cold air or smoke. Anomalies people are convinced are paranormal may be the person's hair that flew in front of the camera at the last minute or a loose finger too close to the lens.

An unusual mist appeared in members' photos, for instance, at a cemetery in Iota.

"I got a strange mist but I can't say it was paranormal," said Broussard. "It could have been moisture in the air."

One piece of evidence that isn't scientific is the feeling one gets in a place that's supposedly haunted. Broussard felt sick and her energy drained at the old sawmill at the Southern Forest Heritage Museum in Forest Hill, and Gardner was freaked out by the Fort Derussy Cemetery in Marksville.

"Nothing in Louisiana scares me, but that place really scared me," Gardner said of Fort Derussy. "I never had an experience, but it's a really creepy place."

To read about the investigations of Louisiana Spirits and hear or view paranormal evidence, visit http://laspirits.com.

CHAPTER 7

THE RICE CAPITAL OF CROWLEY

Charlotte R. Jeffers loves showing off her southwest Louisiana town of Crowley, known for its sprawling rice farms, flamboyant former Louisiana governor Edwin Edwards and a vibrant music heritage. Jeffers's job is tourism coordinator for the city, but her enthusiasm is genuine.

Most of Crowley's ghosts reside in historic buildings, so listening to Jeffers explain the town's apparitions is a lesson in history as well. One thing's for certain, she said: there are no malicious ghosts in Crowley. But then visitors would expect as much from the city "where life is rice and easy."

"I've been doing this for ten years now," Jeffers said of her job promoting Crowley. "Most people want to see ghosts, not the other way around. It's like an attraction. We don't have bad ghosts. We don't have scary ghosts. We have good ghosts."

I met Jeffers at her office, located in the old Ford Motor Company assembly plant at 425 North Parkerson Avenue, the main street through town. The lovely old building dating back to 1921 is now home to City Hall, with four museums on the second floor—the Rice Interpretive Center; the Ford Automotive Museum where two 1923 Model T cars are on display, showcasing how the company once shipped cars in pieces to Crowley and assembled them on the spot; the History of Crowley Museum and the J.D. Miller Music Museum. A rich piece of trivia here is that Crowley songwriter and musician J.D. Miller wrote "It Wasn't God Who Made Honky Tonk Angels," recorded by Kitty Wells, and operated a studio where numerous stars crossed the threshold. Today, J.D.'s son, Mark Miller, runs the studio a

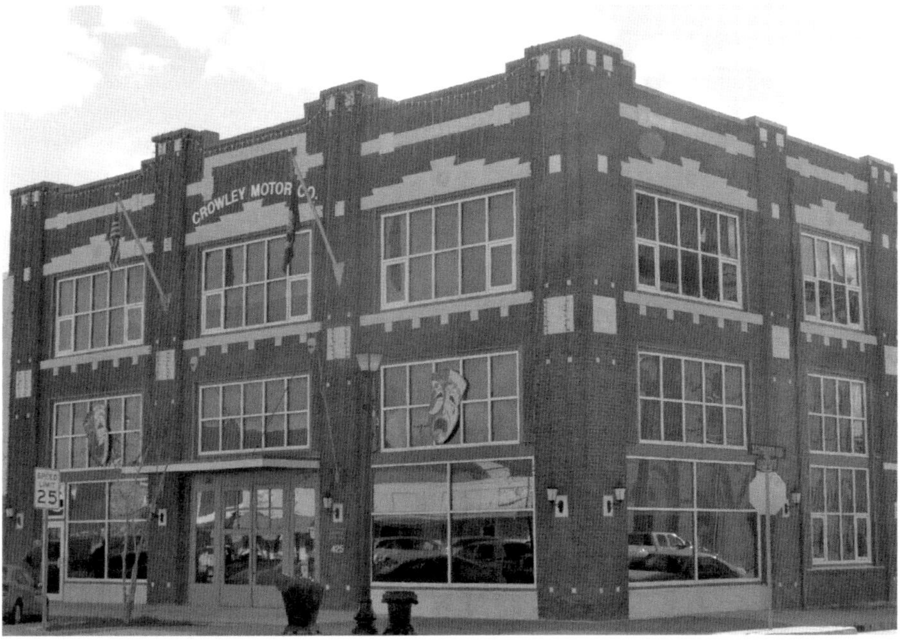

The old Ford Motor Company assembly plant in Crowley is home to the Rice Interpretive Center, the Ford Automotive Museum, the History of Crowley Museum, the J.D. Miller Music Museum and possibly a ghost or two.

few doors down, now known as Master Trak Sound Recorders in the back of Modern Music Center, considered the oldest recording studio in continuous use in the state (see chapter 8).

Joining us the day I met with Jeffers was Marci Lee, a teacher by day and paranormal investigator by night with Louisiana Spirits. Her interest in ghosts dates back to her grandmother's house in Jackson, Mississippi, where a long hallway ended in her grandmother's bedroom. One day after her grandmother had passed, she saw what she thought was her mother heading down the hallway to the back bedroom.

"I saw something go down the hallway to my grandmother's bedroom. When I got in there no one was back there," she said.

Another time at her grandmother's house, her mother felt a blast of cold air at her back and knew someone was behind her, but she was too scared to look around. When she escaped to the living room and told others, they were relieved to hear they were not alone in their experiences.

"Those were the two experiences that got me into ghost hunting and have followed me my whole life," Lee explained.

When Louisiana Spirits offered a leisure class at the University of Louisiana at Lafayette Continuing Education, Lee knew it was time to try her hand at paranormal investigations. The class visited an old home in West Lake near Lake Charles that was once a funeral parlor and caught eerie lights coming in and out of a wall. While Lee was sitting on a bench in the attic, she asked if the spirits would join her and was rewarded with a voice on her recorder saying, "I'm sitting next to you."

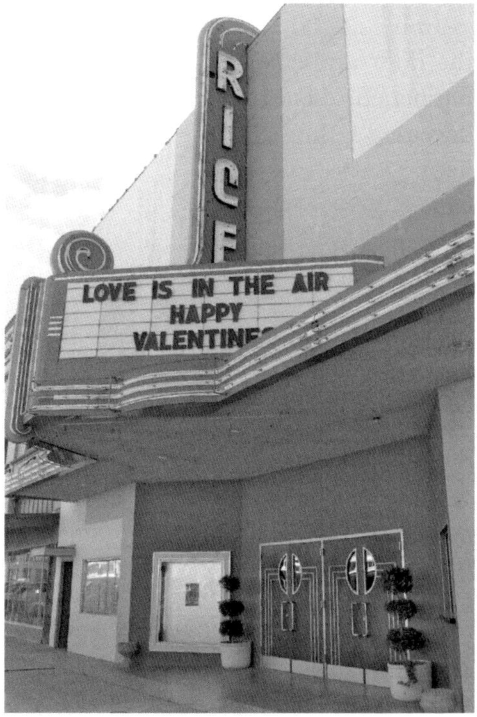

Weird noises and shadows have been reported in the 1941 Rice Theater in Crowley.

Now, she's hooked, performing investigations with the Louisiana Spirits South Central Chapter. And she has lots to say about Crowley.

"In my opinion," Lee said, "Crowley definitely has ghosts."

Jeffers and Lee met when Louisiana Spirits was investigating city hall in the old Ford building and the Rice Theater a few doors down, a 1941 art deco movie theater that has been renovated and is now used for live performances. The investigators didn't pick up paranormal activity at city hall, despite Jeffers's claim that weird noises have been heard and shadows seen in the building.

"They don't always show up," Lee insisted. "You can't make a ghost perform on demand."

At the Rice Theater, however, investigator Chad Gage witnessed a shadow pass through an open door knob, Lee said.

"He said, 'Did you see that? That hole in the door? Someone walked in front of the light,'" Lee related.

The investigators tried to re-create the moment with other scenarios but couldn't do it.

In the Rice Theater's balcony, where African Americans sat during segregation, they asked if this was where blacks were relegated and were treated with the answer, "Yes."

In the sound booth of the old projection room, the investigators opened the door and said, "If you're in here, please shut the door." But nothing happened and the group became inpatient. Lee added, speaking to her deceased father, "Dad, just shut the door so we can leave." Again, nothing happened, and they left. The next day someone from the Rice Theater called Jeffers and asked who shut the door. No one had.

The group also heard a piano note play and a sound like a drum. On the second visit to the Rice Theatre, they caught voices speaking.

Other spots Louisiana Spirits visited in Crowley were the Old Jail, where investigators heard a "shssh" in the women's section and a woman's voice speaking; the Acadia Parish Courthouse where a few bangs were heard; and Mark Miller's studio at Modern Music Center, where the investigator's K-2 meter spiked when they played Kitty Wells singing and which stopped when the music stopped.

Crowley sites Louisiana Spirits hope to visit are the Town Club, where people routinely see a ghost at the bar, and the Old Crowley High (now the Crowley Middle School) where police report unusual things happening.

"People have seen people (the see-through kind) there drinking," Lee said of the Town Club.

CHAPTER 8

WHERE THE MUSIC KEEPS PLAYING

CROWLEY'S MODERN MUSIC CENTER

J.D. "Jay" Miller recorded numerous releases in his Crowley studio, from Kenny Wayne, Paul Simon and John Fogerty to Louisiana Cajun and swamp pop artists.

The Iota native began singing with Cajun and country bands at an early age, receiving his first accolade at the Dairyland Ice Cream Company talent contest at thirteen when he performed "Every Man a King," the anthem of Louisiana governor Huey P. Long. His prize was the chance to perform cowboy tunes on the radio on Saturday mornings.

Miller served in World War II but bouts with malaria forced him to serve as a communication instructor stateside. He and his father operated the M&S Electrical Company at 218 North Parkerson Avenue after the war, but Miller tried his hand at retail with a music store in the corner of the building.

Customers wanted Cajun records, which were hard to find at the time. There were few recording studios in Louisiana postwar, including Cosimo Matassa's in New Orleans and Floyd Soileau's in Ville Platte. Miller started recording Cajun and country artists and did so well that he opened a studio in Crowley. His song "It Wasn't God Who Made Honky Tonk Angels" was recorded by Kitty Wells and flew to number one on the country charts.

Miller's labels included Fais Do-Do, Feature, Zynn, Rocko for rock-n-roll recordings, Showtime and many others.

Today, J.D. Miller's son, Mark Miller, operates Master Trak Sound Recorders studio in the back of Modern Music Center on Parkerson Avenue in downtown Crowley. Through the endless guitars and other

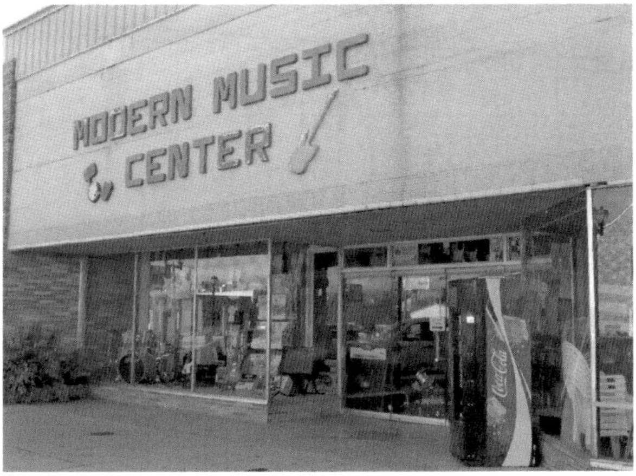

Unexplained events have happened in the music studios of Crowley's Modern Music Center.

instruments hanging from the ceiling, visitors can spot the recording booths toward the rear.

When the studio was originally located between city hall and the present music store, a friend of Mark Miller's went into the booth but failed to find the vocal mic. He asked Mark about it, and the two returned to the booth to find the mic on the floor.

"He didn't look on the floor," Miller recounted. "The mic was on the floor. You have to pull hard to get the mic out of the sleeve."

And then it happened again.

"Another time, a singer came into the recording booth, didn't know about the mic," Miller explained. "He runs out, says 'The mic came out at me!' He didn't know anything about the mic."

When Miller made it inside the recording booth, the mic was again on the floor.

The mic incidents happened when they were renovating the neighboring city hall and the apparition apparently haunting the old Ford Motor Company building decided to travel. "My feeling was the ghost moved," Miller said. "It's just a theory."

Over the years, people have seen apparitions in the studio of the music store, Miller said. On one occasion, Miller heard voices outside the bathroom, but no one was in the building.

"I went all over the building, and no one was there," he said.

A friend saw a male apparition in the tape room, and the description matched Miller's grandfather.

"When the ghost looked at him [his friend], it disappeared," Miller related.

CHAPTER 9
GUESTS WHO REFUSE TO CHECK OUT

CROWLEY'S EGAN HOTEL

Michael Egan and his wife, Jane Healy, came to Crowley from New Orleans in the late nineteenth century with three sons and three daughters. One son, William Michael Egan, opened a rice mill in the nearby Jonas Cove settlement, later called Canal Switch, and the town repaid him by naming the town after him—definitely an improvement over Canal Switch. Egan created a plan of six hundred acres for the establishment of the town of Crowley in 1903, served in the state legislature from 1904 to 1908 and then as mayor of Crowley from 1910 to 1920. On the private side, William Michael Egan was a real estate dealer and insurance agent. He died at the age of fifty-nine on May 22, 1928.

It's unclear if William Egan owned the three-story Egan Hotel in the 300 block of North Parkerson in downtown Crowley. It was built in 1913 at the cost of $34,000 and opened January 1, 1914, with George Dorr as its manager, according to the *Crowley Daily Signal* of December 9, 1913. William's brother Daniel P. Egan owned and operated a hardware and department store at 316 and 318 Parkerson. In the 1920, 1930 and 1940 censuses, another brother, John F. Egan Jr., is listed as a hotel clerk and later hotel assistant manager, although the hotel is not named.

The New Orleans *Times-Picayune* reported on December 11, 1913, that "the Egan Hotel will open Jan. 1 under the management of George Dorr, proprietor of the old Crowley House. The new hotel is a three-story brick building. The lower floor will be occupied by the Rexal Pharmacy, Ogeron's barber shop, Postal Telegraph Company and the hotel lobby."

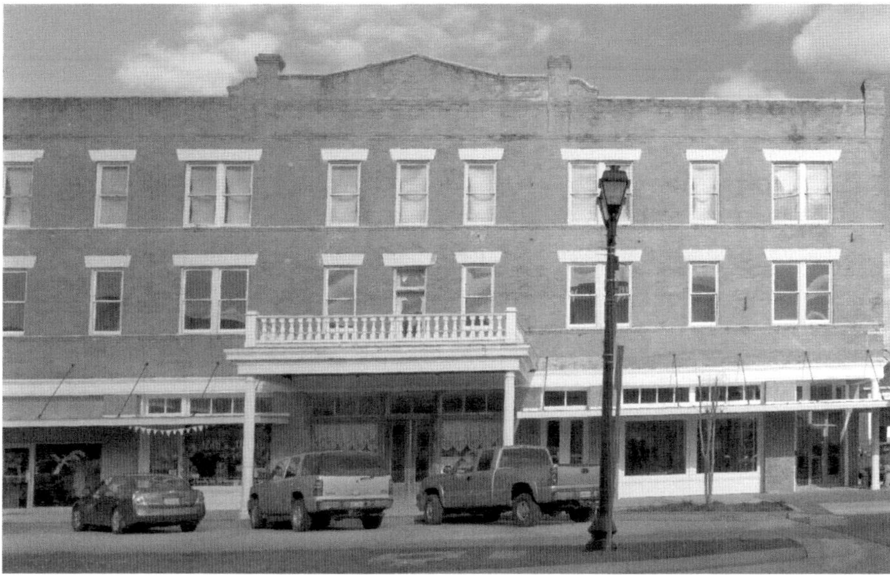

The "creep factor" is high at the old Egan Hotel, say paranormal investigators.

When Mayor William Egan married Phala Baur in a surprise wedding on July 16, 1916, the *New Orleans States* newspaper reported that the couple would "make their home at the Egan Hotel."

The hotel was advertised as a "headquarters for commercial travelers" with "steam heated, hot and cold water" in private baths for $2.50 a night. Famous visitors included Babe Ruth and Clark Gable.

In a 1961 obituary of Mrs. C.A. Peck in the *Morning Advocate* of Baton Rouge, it is claimed that she and her husband "operated the Egan Hotel since 1918." In 1964, the name was changed from the Egan Hotel Inc., Crowley, to Hotel Development Corp. In June and July 1967, an ad was placed in the New Orleans *Times-Picayune* looking for clients to lease the hotel, boasting of restaurant facilities, fifty-two rooms with available TV, air conditioning and steam heat.

Today, the three-story building is being renovated. But stories have circulated for years of its hauntings. Some claim illegal activities occurred in the building, possibly by the mob and possibly involving murder. Another story has it that residents used a Ouiji board that opened a door to another world.

It was with these stories in mind that Louisiana Spirits visited the old hotel.

"Of the many places we have investigated, the Egan Hotel is one of the top as far as grizzly [*sic*] happenings," the paranormal investigators reported on their website. "In its early existence, the hotel was a major mob hangout. That in itself can be assumed for grounds for criminal activity. Reports tell of a young boy and his father being murdered as well as a woman being murdered by her husband. On several occasions, priests have been brought in to perform cleansings of the building. The results of these attempts are small religious medallions being placed over the doors of the rooms where deaths have taken place, only adding to the creep factor."

Little is known about the hotel's history, but one interesting historical tidbit was the discovery of whiskey cases at the Egan Hotel along with the mismanagement of funds by Mayor Egan in the April 4, 1919 *Times-Picayune* of New Orleans:

> *Crowley, La., April 3—Unearthing of whiskey found in all manner of places is being continued by Revenue Officer Douglas and his assistants. Quantities were discovered in many places, from twenty-five cases stored in the Egan Hotel to small amounts in negro shacks. This, coupled with the sensational charges by Alderman John Bethany of the management of the city's affairs, has created much excitement.*
>
> *Alderman Bethany has a long statement in the local daily strongly denouncing the actions of Mayor William Egan.*
>
> *A recent survey of the administration's water and light plant, owned and operated by the city, revealed 240 users of lights at a flat rate of $1.39, who paid nothing at all. The revenue of the city was only $465 per month, when it should have been about $1275.*
>
> *Large crowds gathered at street corners are discussing the city exposure, and larger crowds are following the government officers unearthing and hauling seized whiskey, hidden to avoid the government tax.*

Jennifer Broussard of Louisiana Spirits conducted investigations of the Egan Hotel and picked up interesting EVPs. As she and others were casually discussing visiting the Waffle House for a meal, they heard someone say, "Waffle, waffle, waffle."

"We get our best EVPs when we're not trying," Broussard explained.

Other paranormal elements the group detected in the Egan Hotel were numerous EMF spikes in Room 302 with the K-2 meter; a major EMF spike in Room 207; two EMF fluctuations in Room 14; knocks in Room 232 when asked for a sign; tall shadows, banging and a childlike noise laughing and cooing on the second floor; thermometer drops when asked; and a voice saying, "My pleasure" caught on tape when the group thanked them for the experience.

CHAPTER 10

GHOSTS ON STAGE

THE GRAND OPERA HOUSE OF THE SOUTH

Kim Gattle and her mother, Carol "Che Che" Gielen, are quick to point out that they've never seen a ghost at the Grand Opera House of the South even though the old entertainment venue in the heart of Crowley used for live performances, vaudeville and Hollywood movies is reportedly very haunted.

Regardless, the mother and daughter sure have had their experiences.

Che Che and her husband, Lazar John "L.J." Gielen, bought the old theater in 1999. At the time, the downstairs housed Dixie Hardware and a gift shop while the upstairs theater space was used for storage. When the couple purchased the business, they agreed to keep the hardware store going until the former owners' family retired or passed on.

In 2004, after keeping their promise, the Gielens formed a nonprofit organization to restore the building and bring the theater back to its former glory. They knew what was behind the storage boxes—a magnificent theater with protruding, elegant box seats, painted murals in robin's egg blue and gold leaf and a grand staircase cascading down the building's center. All the theater needed was some tender loving care and several million dollars.

In 2008, Dixie Hardware closed and the Grand Opera House reopened. The eloquent theater has been a local favorite for weddings and special events, plus live performances, ever since.

The origins of the grand theater hail back to 1901, when a twenty-nine-year-old stable owner and deputy sheriff by the name of David Lyons dreamed of a theater to attract major acts to Crowley, a town halfway

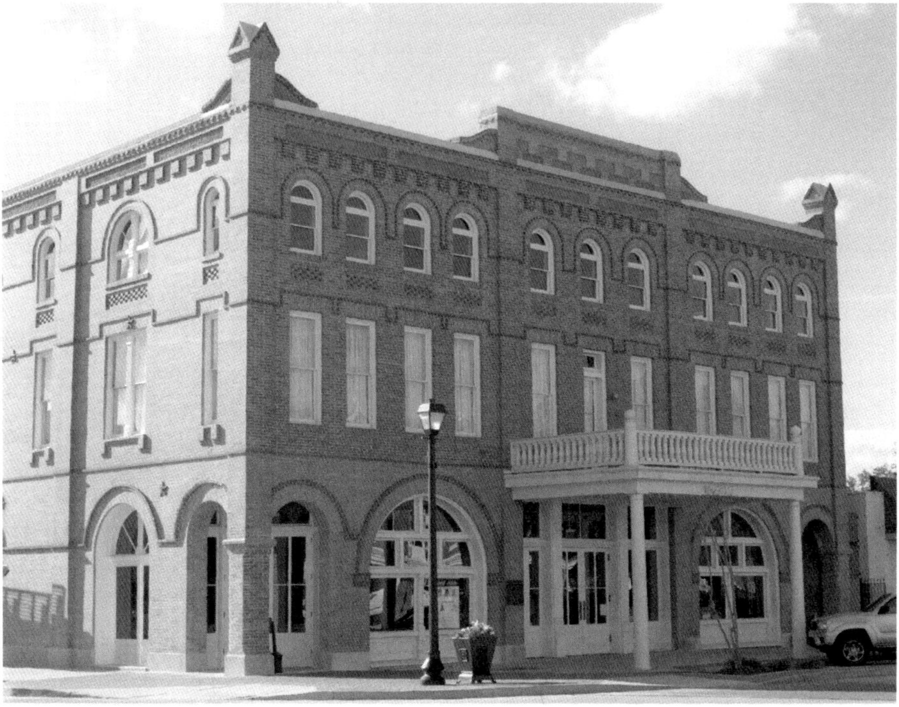

Numerous spirits still linger at the majestic Grand Opera House of the South in downtown Crowley.

between New Orleans and Houston on a railroad line. He envisioned a staircase leading up to the theater, where visitors would take their seats and look down on the stage. On the ground floor would be retail space opening onto the busiest street in Crowley.

In total, the building cost him $18,000, and Lyons lived as a lifelong bachelor in an apartment next to his office space on the second floor.

The theater indeed attracted performers, from vaudeville and minstrel shows to silent movies and concerts. Of the celebrities who have graced the stage were Babe Ruth, Clark Gable and opera singers Enrico Caruso and Madame de Vilchez-Bisset of the Paris Opera. During an election year, flamboyant Louisiana governor Huey P. Long filled the room with his "Every Man a King" political rhetoric.

The theater was also used for various civic events, such as the 1904 graduation ceremonies of Crowley High School. At one point in the graduation, Rose Wilder stood up and read Edgar Allan Poe's "The Raven" in Latin. Rose was the daughter of Laura Ingalls Wilder and the one who had encouraged her mother to pen her *Little House on the Prairie* tales of childhood. Rose Wilder had come to live with her aunt, Eliza Jane Wilder Thayer Gordon of Crowley, and to finish school.

Over the years, the ground floor beneath the magnificent theater that attracted such famous names had housed a saloon, café, bakery, pool hall and town mortuary until Dixie Hardware took the location.

Opulent theaters so popular in the early twentieth century eventually fell out of favor and the Grand Opera House was no exception. By the time Dixie Hardware occupied the building, the theater space hiding behind mounds of storage was in bad need of a facelift.

The Gielens poured $4.5 million into the theater over a period of years to bring the old lady back under the direction of award-winning architect Donald J. Breaux. It now sits among the more than two hundred structures in Crowley that are listed on the National Register of Historic Places, with Kim Gattle as its executive director.

As mother and daughter attest, they have never seen an apparition. And yet they spent two hours one winter day regaling me with stories.

Did They Really Break a Leg?

It all started with Dixie Hardware. The Gielens first heard of the building's ghosts after they had purchased the business and the theater lurking behind the boxes. Customers routinely claimed to have seen an ethereal man and woman within the store, Che Che Gielen said, and the former owner related how he used to squeeze in some exercise by walking up and down the back staircase, until something or someone pushed him from behind.

"He [the former owner] said all the hairs on the back of his head would stand up," Gielen said.

Another time, Gielen heard loud cracks coming from the front of the store. On arrival, she found glass shelves broken as if they had popped up and shattered. The strangest sight, however, were the china pieces and the glass chimneys for hurricane lanterns lying all over the floor in perfect shape, not a scratch on them.

"The shelf would break, but it was never damaging," Gielen explained. "It never hurt anybody."

Both Che Che and her husband received an "ice cold wind" in the dressing room one day, a sensation they couldn't explain, and one that gave them chills in more ways than one.

Since the closure of Dixie Hardware, Gattle has spent endless hours on the property, first in the building's reconstruction and then to oversee weddings and special events or rehearsals and performances within the theater. She was at a wedding rehearsal once, setting up for the reception downstairs while the wedding photographer was on stage inside the theater. Weird lights and haze kept appearing on his photos, making him extremely anxious.

"I said, 'Is everything going all right?' And he said, 'I'm about to throw up,'" Gattle recalled.

Gattle explained about the opera house's ghostly "friends" and told the photographer to politely tell them to leave him alone and let him take his photos.

They did.

"I left and he had a little talk," she said. "Almost immediately his pictures changed."

When Gattle was setting up lights for a wedding to be held on the stage, her father, L.J. Gielen, came in, and the whole theater went black. He fussed at the ghosts, and the lights came back on.

At another wedding, the florist told Gattle she witnessed a ghostly woman in a white dress within the theater. But it was a child that was keeping her from doing her work. A little boy about three to four years old would not leave her alone, she told Gattle, insisting that he wanted to play. Gattle imparted to her the same instructions she gave the photographer. The florist talked to the boy and told him she needed to work, and he left. Gattle said she later felt bad for the ghost because the boy just wanted to play.

Other people have seen the lady in the white dress. One woman who wished not to be named (let's call her Carol) described the ghost as having her hair pulled back in a bun standing in the area that now houses the opera house museum on the second floor. She was smiling and appeared to have a nice countenance, the woman said. The lady in white also related to Carol how happy she was with the crucifix hung above one of the museum doors.

Carol also claimed a little girl followed her around and that a ghost of a man lurked in the theater.

Once when Carol visited for an Irma Thomas concert, the woman in white met her downstairs, brought her to the museum and showed her flowers, Gattle said. Another time, Gattle was taking a family photo on the stage, and Carol claimed the woman in white was behind them.

When Kim's daughter used to visit the theater, she also saw the woman in white. But she didn't like going upstairs because of the children, Gattle said. On the other hand, when Gielen's granddaughter visited from Houston as a child she had an imaginary friend named "Boo" on the second floor and always wanted to visit him. Now that she's in high school, "She can't see him no longer," Gielen explained. And Kim's daughter doesn't see the ghosts anymore either.

When the Lowe family from Branson came to perform at the Grand Opera House, Gattle heard children playing within the building, so she immediately thought they were the Lowes' grandchildren. When she asked the family members where the children were, the family said they hadn't come. That night the performance included streamers and confetti, and when Gattle, her husband and Gielen were cleaning up, Gattle kept hearing the kids playing again. Her husband insisted it was a cat, but Gattle knew better. She went to get her purse and heard "Mom!" exclaimed from the second floor so loud that she and her mother both jumped.

"As clear as day, like a child four to five years old," Gattle said.

She and her mother took off running, locked the door and headed for home. Since her mother had heard the child's voice too, Gattle felt vindicated.

"She was so glad I heard it too," Gielen said.

There's a story that an African American man hanged himself on stage, apparently after a card game went terribly wrong. There's even a piece of the rope on display within the museum. Many people see a man in the theater, sometimes on the balcony, and some believe it's the ghost of Mr. Lyons.

Charlotte Jeffers, tourism coordinator for the city of Crowley, brought two visiting couples into the historic building one day, and Gielen gave them a tour. Gielen led them into the theater and flicked on the lights.

"All of a sudden Charlotte screamed," Gielen related. "She said someone was in the bleachers. He ducked as if to hide. She said 'I saw what I saw.'"

During the theater's reconstruction, Gattle was on the third floor with an elevator inspector. Suddenly, the elevator started from below and arrived empty at their floor. Gattle laughed and blamed it on the Opera House's ghosts, to which the man replied, "You have them!" He claimed to have seen a Caucasian man about six feet, two inches tall in the middle aisle of the theater turn slowly around and look at him.

"He said he liked to hang out by this railing, going up and down the staircase," Gattle explained what the elevator inspector had said. "When we started construction in December, several years ago, he [the elevator inspector] didn't see him again."

One man doing electrical work within the theater kept finding his shoelaces untied on his left boot. He went into a nook and found a pair of boots with the left boot's shoelaces untied.

An electrical engineer came in, crawling into the theater's nooks and crannies to take photos under the bleachers. When she later examined the photos she found that one was of her, "as if she had turned the camera and took a picture of her face," Gattle said.

Another time two workers were working on the second-floor rooms, removing a wall. They attempted to move a Lazy Boy chair from the room and found it wouldn't budge. Then the lights went out. The pair freaked and fled downstairs, relating their experience to Gattle's father. Upon hearing the tale, another worker laughed, went up to the second-floor room and easily picked up the chair.

The movie projection box has a tin flap attached, and one day, it was flapping of its own accord. A worker in the projection box came down and asked who was playing games with him. But no one had been up there.

People who have performed in plays or who have visited the theater for special events have seen the theater's ghosts. Sara Fox was working with a local television station for a Halloween taping and knew things were about to get interesting.

"I said don't be surprised if your cameras don't work," she said.

The mic wouldn't turn on, so they tried new batteries. That didn't solve the problem. Fox then tried the lapel mic, and it didn't work either. Then they tried the camera mic. Frustrated, the reporter finally went outside to attempt a recording. Once away from the theater, everything worked fine.

Even the family dog has had experiences. Gypsy would run around the theater as if it was chasing something, Gattle explained. Sometimes it would run in circles on the stage.

"You couldn't tell if she was chasing the ghosts or they were chasing her," Gattle said with a laugh.

Who Haunts the Grand Opera House?

The original owner, David E. Lyons, lived on the second floor of the Grand Opera House. He never married and apparently had a mistress. In the 1930 census, Lyons is listed with two African American "helpers," Mary Smith and Joe Brown, plus Nonie Perry, a widowed woman listed as his secretary. A

Lyons cousin once told Gattle that she was never allowed in Lyons's bedroom because he had money stashed there and a loaded gun.

Lyons died April 4, 1940, at the age of seventy-six, according to Louisiana death records.

Perhaps the male ghost haunting the theater is that of Dave Lyons. Or perhaps it's the man who committed suicide on stage, distraught over losing all his money in a card game. The woman in white could be Lyons's mistress or a Catholic actress who longs for an armful of flowers for one more curtain call.

As for the children, it's anyone's guess.

One thing Gattle and Gielen know for certain: the ghosts of the Grand Opera House are nice spirits.

"We've never had any negative things happen," Gattle said.

When things take a funny turn, such as an invisible hand repeatedly hitting one key on her computer screen, so that her computer desktop is filled with an endless letter of the alphabet, Gattle tells them to stop, that she has work to do, and they oblige.

"I think they want to remind us they are the boss of the building," Kim said.

Chapter 11

The Raymond Thurston Clark House

Dr. Dale Leleux hails from Lyons Point near Crowley. When he and his wife, Christy, were looking to relocate from Baton Rouge not too long after Hurricane Katrina had whipped through the state in 2005, it was natural for them to consider his hometown. They had spotted a house that met their approval, but the owners were asking more than they cared to spend; prices were unnaturally high due to New Orleans residents seeking refuge from the storm.

Their realtor mentioned the Miller House on Second Street in downtown Crowley, a Queen Anne beauty that had been on the market for a considerable time. Dr. Leleux had loved that house ever since he was a kid and was excited about touring the inside.

The home wasn't in the best shape, however. It had long been unoccupied except for an occasional renter. Dr. Leleux's brother-in-law worked for the Sheriff's Office and knew some of the workers who had lived there for a time. Even though many of Leleux's friends had raved about the three-story home built before the turn of the twentieth century, calling it "magnificent," the Leleuxes were not impressed once they toured the Victorian relic.

"We expected the insides to be museum quality," Christy Leleux said. "It was run down. We were in and out in like ten minutes."

In fact, Dr. Leleux couldn't wait to leave.

"After we left, Dale said, 'I was so disappointed, I felt like I had to go home and take a shower,'" Christy Leleux recounted. "He said something's wrong, felt like he had to go to church or something."

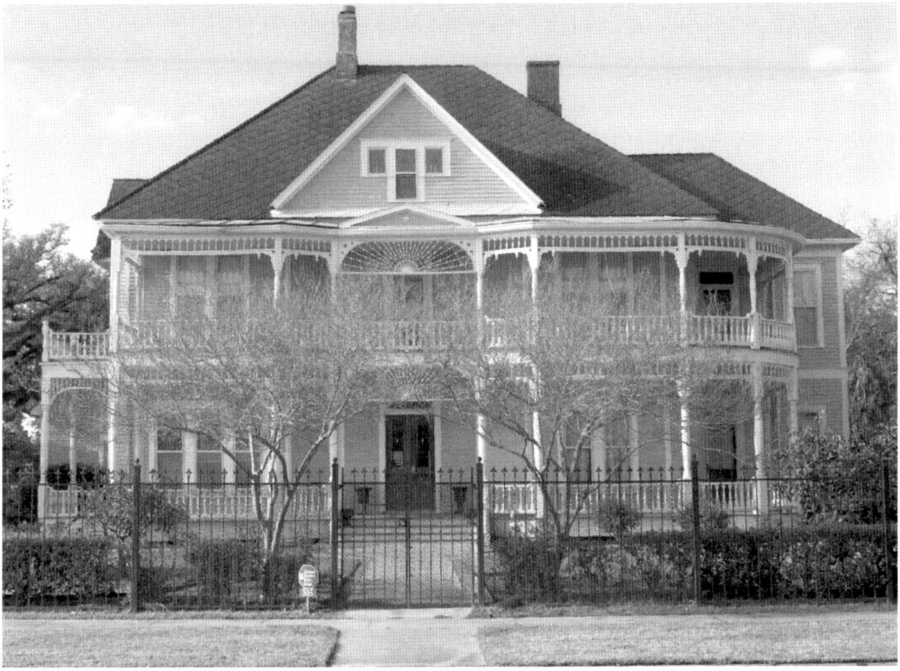

The stately Raymond Thurston Clark Home in Crowley has had lots of paranormal activity, including weird events on the third floor.

Time passed, and the owner of the first house, the one they had loved and bid on, hadn't budged in his price. Again, the realtor mentioned the Miller House. The Leleuxes decided to take a second look.

"Physically, nothing had changed," Leleux said. "It still looked like nobody lived there. But we agreed to look at it with a new pair of eyes."

To both their surprise, the house was more appealing.

"Dale felt better about it," Leleux said. "It was like 180 degrees from when we first visited the house."

In their second tour, they found a devotional scapular wrapped around a doorknob, and Dr. Leleux insisted it hadn't been there the first time. Apparently between the first and second visit, the house had been blessed.

"It was a completely different feeling to this house," Leleux explained. "The first time Dale was not "No" but "Hell no!" to the house."

The couple decided to purchase the old Miller House, and they moved in with their three children.

First, the Clark Family

The Leleuxes bought the house on West Second Street from Jack Miller, a Crowley attorney, but the three-story Victorian home dates back to 1898. Acadia Parish judge Raymond Thurston Clark built the Queen Anne home with Eastlake galleries filled with ten large rooms, a first-floor parlor and a third-floor attic space.

Both Judge Clark and his wife were prominent citizens of Crowley. The son of an Acadia Parish cattle rancher and planter, Clark went into business as a rancher near Rayne and later served as a Rayne councilman. He married Laura L. Duson on December 17, 1874, the youngest daughter of Cornelius Duson and Sarah Ann Webb. Laura's brother Cornelius C. "Curley" Duson served as a legendary lawman, a Louisiana senator, a major mover in the development of Acadia Parish (Eunice, Louisiana, was named for his wife, Mary Eunice Pharr Duson) and as a U.S. marshal in 1906, appointed by President Theodore Roosevelt. Raymond T. Clark served as a justice of the peace and was Acadia Parish's first clerk of court. He was "an unwavering democrat," according to *Southwest Louisiana Biographical and Historical*, edited by William Henry Perrin in 1891, and was a member of the Methodist Church, Knights of Pythias (of which Louis Armstrong and Franklin D. Roosevelt were members) and Knights of Honor, a fraternal organization.

The *Crowley Signal* newspaper of October 27, 1894, wrote this about Judge Clark:

> *R.T. Clark has served the people of Acadia in the recorder and Clerk of Court since the inception of a parochial government in 1887, and nothing could speak in louder praise of his executive ability and universal popularity than the fact that he has been twice reelected by the people to the office.*
>
> *Judge Clark was born on April 23, 1855, at Plaquemine Brulee in this parish, and was raised on the farm. In his early years he attended the neighborhood schools, but went to Opelousas later and entered a boarding school under the supervision of Rev. C.A. Frazee. He engaged in farming and stock raising for a number of years, but was elected justice of the peace in 1884 and removed to Rayne in the same year. He was elected Clerk of Court in March of 1887, and was reelected in 1888 and again in 1892. In the spring of '88 he removed his family to Crowley and has since made this his home.*

The Clark family moved into the large house with their children (as reported in the 1900 census, listing oldest to youngest) Leonard H. Clark, Eunice Estelle Clark, Eula F. Clark, Lillian T. Clark, Vivian S. Clark, Hilda T. Clark, V. Cornelius Clark, Susan Viola Clark and Raymond T. Clark Jr. Of the children, Leonard, Eula and Lillian are reported as attending school.

On November 7, 1900, Estelle Clark married Dr. Manassa L. Hoffpauir with Lillian as a bridesmaid and Eula as maid of honor.

In the 1910 census, Raymond and Laura Clark are listed with their children Hilda Clark, "Con" Clark, Susie Clark, R.T. Clark Jr. and Mrs. John Dugan, a servant. Cornelius is listed as working for the rice mill, while Susie, Hilda and Raymond Jr. have no occupation.

Raymond T. Clark Sr. died on September 25, 1911, leaving behind a widow to care for her many children.

Eula F. Clark married Fleet Coleman. Sue Clark married William Beatty Cleveland on January 24, 1920, with Hilda as a maid of honor and Eula as matron of honor.

By the 1930 census, it's clear the Depression or lack of a husband's income had taken its toll on the Clark family, for Laura Clark and her daughter Hilda are living in the house on Second Street along with both servants and lodgers. Sue Clark Cleveland is also residing in the home with her two daughters: Sue Clark, age nine, and Jane, age seven.

An article appearing in the August 30, 1936 *Times-Picayune* of New Orleans reported, "Miss Hilda Clark entertained at an outdoor steak fry in compliment to her niece, Miss Jane Cleveland of Memphis, Tenn., who is visiting relatives in Crowley." The party was held at the home on Second Street.

In the 1940 census, Hilda Clark remains at the house, along with J.F. Coleman, "clean rice man, married"; her sister Eula Coleman; and lodgers Harvey Fuselier, T.B. McMilbarn and Mildred Wade. Sister Estelle Hoffpauir lives next door at 320 West Second Street with son Clark and daughter Dorothy and grandchildren Jack, Clark and William.

In July 1976, Hilda Clark died.

The home passed to three more owners until the Leleuxes: a New Orleans doctor and his wife who only lived there a short time—according to Leleux—a Dr. Alfred Harmon and, finally, Jack Miller.

Up until the closing, the Leleuxs had heard mention that the house contained more than brick and mortar. Jack Miller added to the mystery by going back and forth, first telling them it was haunted and then following up with, "Just kidding," Leleux said. Some claimed the ghost stories involved a disabled young boy who had been shut in on the third floor. He had been taken to the second-floor balcony for fresh air and fallen over. Another story had a young girl whose nightshirt caught on fire and who was killed.

"Everyone's got their own version of the story," Leleux said, but almost all contend that the child was of toddler age and was kept secluded on the third floor.

Miller did parlay to the Leleuxes the time he hired a couple to do carpentry work on the house. Because the couple was from out of town, they spent the night at the Crowley estate. One morning Miller showed up at the house only to find them sitting on the porch, refusing to work there anymore. They claimed the place was haunted and left for good.

Dr. Leleux's brother worked in the Acadia Parish Sheriff's Department, and one of his co-workers had rented a room in the Miller House for a time. The worker warned the Leleuxes not to buy the house, claiming it was haunted.

"He wouldn't go to the third floor," Leleux added.

But buy they did.

Christy Leleux moved in with her children. Dr. Leleux was still working in Baton Rouge, and their Capital City house had yet to be sold. Many nights during those early days Christy slept alone in the old Victorian. Ancient houses take some getting used to, from the air conditioner that rattles like a heavy sigh to the general settling of wood as temperatures drop in the night. With a large house more than one hundred years old, there can be myriad noises.

"I had to learn the new sounds before they freaked me out," she said.

One sound she had difficulty getting used to was that of a young child sobbing in the night. Leleux calls it the "sobs sobs," when a child sucks in breath at the end of a crying spree. Because her children were young, she had "Mama's brain," waking up at the smallest noise, so she heard the sobbing on many occasions. The toddler's crying ceased in the daytime, but then her children's waking noise would drown out anything, she added with a smile.

"I would hear it periodically and always at night," she related. "Its sobbing always sounded like pain, like something happened."

One night, she was giving her daughter a bottle downstairs and the crying commenced. She knew then that it wasn't her nighttime imagination getting the best of her or that of a dream. At the time, her son also mentioned a little boy in the house and called him his friend.

A friend of Christy advised her to visit the third floor and tell the toddler that it was okay to be in the house but the crying had to stop. Christy needed her sleep.

"And like an idiot I did," she recalled with a laugh. "I said, 'You need to go.' And I never heard it again."

Devil's Advocate

Christy Leleux doesn't disbelieve in the ghosts in her house, but she doesn't claim it's haunted either. Most of the strange activities that have happened at the Second Street home she could chalk up to the kids or an old house settling or reacting to wind or movement.

"I'm open to it and the devil's advocate," she said. "I have to justify everything to keep me from going crazy."

For instance, one morning she woke up and the front door was wide open. It could have been the kids rushing out without thinking or the old lock refusing to work properly. Or maybe it was something more ethereal heading across the threshold. Leleux had no explanation.

Another time Leleux unloaded the dishwater to find the plastic containers still wet. She quickly placed them on the kitchen counter to dry and turned to perform another chore when one of the cups went flying off the countertop. She tried to justify the event, that maybe the cup was placed in haste and shifted. But she reiterated that it "flew" off the counter.

"It's not scary," she said of the unexplained events happening in her house. "Nothing's weird enough to finish me off."

She and the children joke that the "ghost did it" when a light is left on or a door left ajar.

"I can guarantee I've walked up the stairs and turned off lights and gone back up, and they were on," she said. "But other than little things like lights or doors—and I've had plenty with my kids—we've never had anything scary happen"—unless you can count her daughter's mysterious visit to the third floor.

The Third Floor

The Leleux family renovated the first two floors of their house for family use but left the third floor—its walls covered in mirrors from when Jack Miller used it as a gym—for storage space. Dr. Leleux worries about his patients' privacy so the computer with his business information is kept far away from the kids, on the third floor amid the boxes.

One night, Christy and Dale Leleux went out, leaving the kids alone with a babysitter. All four—three children and the babysitter—were in the second-floor playroom. The boys were playing video games and the baby resting when the oven buzzer sounded.

"She [the babysitter] said to the boys, 'Guys, watch your sister. I'm going to get the pizza out of the oven,'" Leleux said.

The sitter took the back stairs to the kitchen, pulled the pizza out, placed it on top of the stove and quickly rejoined the kids. Only the youngest, who was about ten months at the time, was nowhere to be found. The sitter immediately checked the main staircase but no baby. She came back into the room and quizzed the boys, but they hadn't a clue.

Then she heard laughter coming from the third floor.

The sitter raced up the stairs to find the baby sitting in front of the computer, happily playing with the keyboard and laughing. She was retrieved and brought back to the second-floor playroom, but no one can explain how she climbed up the more than twenty steps to the third floor, maneuvered her way through storage and climbed up into a chair within the time it took the sitter to rush to the kitchen and pull a pizza out of the oven.

And the baby wasn't walking yet.

"She would have had to crawl up the staircase to the third floor and finagle her way to the back computer and into the chair," Leleux said. "We don't know what happened. If you ask the boys they have no recollection of her leaving the room."

To this day, Leleux doesn't want to envision her child levitating up the stairs at the hands of a ghost, but she keeps asking, "How did she get up there?"

Third Party Reports

Construction workers at the property had a few strange events to report. A worker in the sunroom left the house to wash his paintbrushes outside in the hose. He heard old-fashioned music playing within the house, but once he came back inside, the music ceased. Leleux likened his experience to the baby crying.

"It was like a faded sound, but it was definitely there," she said.

Another time, a worker had left the poolside, pulling the pool's iron gate door shut behind him. The gate would vibrate some after the gate closed and did this day like any other. The worker leaned over to perform a task when the gate opened and closed again. Thinking it was another worker, he straightened and turned around to find no one there. But the gate was vibrating once again.

"He said the gate was moving as if it'd been shut a second time," Leleux explained. "And he said no one came out after him. He said, 'You have ghosts in your house,' straight out."

INVESTIGATION

Louisiana Spirits paranormal investigators approached the Leleuxes about performing an investigation in the house. The family agreed, and the team arrived one night with armfuls of equipment. They visited the infamous third floor but "nothing blatant happened," Leleux said.

The first-floor parlor was another story.

Christy Leleux rested in a chair while the team members sat nearby, and all were relaxed and "chit chatty," Leleux said. It was a chilly night and the home's heaters had been shut off because they made too much noise.

One of the team members suddenly got very cold.

To test if the sudden chill might be a wind blowing from underneath the house, investigator Marci Lee put a thermometer between them and let it settle to sixty-seven degrees.

"All of a sudden the temperature gauge starts fluctuating," Leleux said. "It starts going down really slow."

The team concluded that wind under the house would have made the thermometer react more dramatically.

"It continued to go down," Leleux said. "By this point, it was sixty-six point something. Marci said, 'I want you to impress us, bring it down to sixty-four.'"

The thermometer then went down at a "steady pace" and stopped at sixty-four.

"The hairs on my entire body were standing up," Leleux explained. "Marci said, 'Okay, that's good.' And it went back up to sixty-seven. That was the most convincing part of the night for me."

Also in the parlor when they were cutting up, Lee said, "Come on, we're having a good time." When they later listened to the conversation, a man's voice replies with an old-time Southern drawl, "I'm sitting right here." There was a male investigator in the room at the time, but if he had spoken up, Lee would have paused. In the recording, the unexplained voice speaks while Lee is talking.

"We probably listened to that a hundred times," Leleux said, adding that she pictures the apparition as a man in his thirties, a Southern gentleman.

Afterward, the group visited the second floor, Christy in the foyer and the others in the bedrooms. Trains kept traveling by, belting out noises in the night and messing up the group's recordings. At one point they all started laughing and someone said sarcastically, "Oh guys, what's that?" and laughed. On the recording a child answers excitedly, "It's a train!"

"It's really clear," Leleux said. "It's not an adult voice."

After the investigation, one of her children heard them discussing the ghosts. Until that time, the parents had worked to keep the ghost stories from their children's ears.

"He said he didn't like the third floor," Leleux said. "He said it freaked him out, that he got a weird feeling there and heard footsteps up and down the stairs."

Louisiana Spirits investigators claim ghosts appear more frequently when their homes are disrupted. The Leleuxes plan to call the paranormal team back on their next construction project.

Who Haunts the Clark House?

No record of the Clark family exists until the 1900 census, and all those children listed are too old to be the toddler on the third floor. Could a child have been born to the Clarks, kept out of the public eye and died before 1900?

The biographical information on Raymond Clark reported in *Southwest Louisiana Biographical and Historical* of 1891 reports that he had eight children, six sons and two daughters. According to the 1900 census, the Clarks actually had nine children, three sons and six daughters.

After the death of Judge Clark, his wife and daughter Hilda took in boarders. Since Crowley was home to a minor league baseball team, ironically named the Crowley Millers, traveling team members stayed at the Clark home.

When Eunice Amy married Frank Bacon in 1924, they moved into "Miss Hilda Clark's on Second Street," wrote Mrs. Bacon in the Acadia Genealogical and Historical Society newsletter. "Miss Hilda had only men roomers. But Frank persuaded her that she should make an exception in our case—so I became the first woman roomer in the Clark home."

It's possible the toddler wasn't even a member of the Clark family. There was a Crowley child burned to death after her clothes caught on fire standing in front of an open fireplace, but she was nine-year-old Ida Marks, daughter of Mr. and Mrs. J.D. Marks. The incident happened in December 1904.

Leleux has done research into the history of the house but can make no clear connection. She also wonders if spirits are attached to antiques she has purchased. One thing's for certain: her house has seen numerous events since its inception in the nineteenth century.

"At that time people died in the house, they had funerals in the house, people were born in the house," she said.

Leleux doesn't mind that ethereal people reside in her home. Her only fear is for the safety of her children. Should anything paranormal become harmful to her kids, it's time to move, she said. So far, nothing, whether live or in the spirit world, has been threatening, but there have been times when Leleux has wondered.

For instance, there was a time when her middle son experienced night terrors, fear so intense Leleux would find him sweating and screaming but still sound asleep. Every time she would awake to his screams, she would head down the hall to his bedroom, her stomach in knots, praying she wouldn't find her child pinned to his bed by unseen hands.

"It was the only time my brain went in that direction," she said. "But they [the night terrors] stopped as soon as they started."

Like the time the Leleuxes visited the home a second time and found it much more appealing, so do visitors. When the babysitter in question visited with two of her friends, girls who had visited the house years prior when the Millers lived there, they began recounting eerie stories of their youth.

"One of them said the house scared her, and it didn't feel right but now it feels right," Leleux said. "She said she definitely had a different feeling when she walked in the house."

And that gives Christy Leleux comfort.

THE NURSE WHO NEVER LEFT

Dr. Leleux owns a practice in nearby Kaplan, one he is purchasing from longtime physician Dr. Carl Richard. With the business came something he never expected—a nurse in full uniform who is long dead.

Those who have worked in his office have complained of items being mixed up in cabinets and images passing by in their periphery. It was enough to call in Louisiana Spirits for an investigation.

"The girls who work there swear they see spirits; but we went there with Louisiana Spirits, and we picked up nothing," Christy Leleux said.

One day someone in a white coat walked by and Dr. Leleux immediately thought it was Dr. Richard. When asked where he was, staff members said he wasn't there that day. Dr. Leleux insisted he saw someone dressed in a white jacket.

"The others said that's what we've been saying all the time," Christy Leleux said.

Dr. Leleux's aunt cleans the office and one weekend had her husband drive her in. As the husband was sitting in the lobby reading, the wife took to mopping the floors. The next thing she knew, the floors were muddy with footprints. She fussed at her husband, but he insisted he never moved from his chair.

People in Kaplan believe it to be a nurse who once worked at the clinic, which explains the uniform. As for not appearing when Louisiana Spirits visited, she might have shied away from attention, preferring to show herself during the hustle and bustle of a physician's office.

"If she worked there she would have been more comfortable with patients there," Leleux explained. "But I was kinda bummed."

CHAPTER 12
LE MAUVAIS HOMME DU MARAIS BOULEUR

OR, THE BAD MEN OF MARAIS BOULEUR

The following is a submitted story by Viola Fontenot regarding a little known area called Marais Bouleur, north of the city of Lafayette. It was once a swampy region that attracted lawlessness and murder.

As Cajun folklore goes, there are a lot of different stories about the bad men of the Marais Bouleur area. The French word *marais* is described as a low, hollow area that collects water, like a marsh.

The Reverend Donald J. Hebert wrote in *The History of the Church at Marais Bouleur, Mire, Louisiana*, which covers its history from 1872 to 1991, that the community went from the name Marais Bouleur to Bosco to Mire and at times included Cankton and Castille. According to Hebert, the name Marais Bouleur stems from a story about a horse named Bouleur who liked to roll in the mud of the swampy wetlands. Since there were no written records or documents about Marais Bouleur, Hebert relied on "the memories of the older generation."

The Marais Bouleur area can be described as that area just northeast of Mire, a swampy area that remains wet most of the year. There is a gravel road, north of Mire, not quite a mile on the right side of Highway 95, known as the Marais Bouleur Road. On both sides of this road is what was always referred to as *Le Marais Bouleur*.

"The expression '*les batailleurs du Marais Bouleur*' expresses, in a way, the temperament of some of those who gained notoriety, and in turn gave the Marais Bouleur section such a bad reputation," writes Hebert. "This quarrelsome, aggressive, daring, even fighting attitude was just a part of the country life. The isolation and seclusion created something of a 'backwards' legacy. A legacy of knives, shootings, fightings, daring gestures, such as the cutting off of someone's necktie and pinning it on the wall; just a daring kind of people. The stories of entering a dance hall and sticking one's knife on the wall to hang a hat there (making it easier to find their knife if a fight started) were all part of this daring attitude. One observation mentioned was that part of the men's preparation for going out to a dance on Saturday night was the usual sharpening of the knives. They just loved their knives."

Pat Bourque from one of my French Tables (a "French Table" in Lafayette is a gathering of French-speaking individuals who meet regularly for French conversation and company) related to me that the family names of the early settlers such as Lyons, Meche, Bergeron, Melancon and others were linked to the "*Le Mauvais Homme du Marais Bouleur*." He also told me a story handed down from his father-in-law, Walker Lyons: "Back in those days, one prescribed manner of fighting was that a circle be drawn around the two fighters, each holding a knife in his hand, then the fighters' hands were tied together by a handkerchief before they started the fight."

"These stories and the people behind them certainly [do] not speak for all of Marais Bouleur, but their escapades certainly brought about a well known and accepted fact, 'be careful of the *batailleurs* [fighters] du Marais Bouleur,'" wrote Hebert.

Hebert relates a story about Tit-Homer Meche, one of the *mauvais homme* or "bad men." "It is said that he could shoot and kill a crow in flight with a pistol; he could strike a large kitchen match at some distance with his revolver and ignite the match…just to name a few," wrote Hebert. "There were others besides him that had such nervy and daring attitudes, but he was one of the most celebrated. So many individuals were involved in criminal acts and lawlessness; there were so many killings, some by knife, some by pistol, and some by such objects such as fence post, a stove, anything that could hurt and maim.

"Many of the persons who committed these acts of violence were related to each other," he added.

For instance, on Sept. 10, 1904, William Bruner and Joseph Neville were found murdered at Coulee Croche, shot by the nineteen-year-old Homer Meche. The actual killings took place across the road from Ernest Higginbotham's store, under the large oak tree where a bar was located. According to Acadia Parish courthouse records the trial against Meche began on Dec. 5, 1905. Family tales claim he spent thirty years or so in Angola State Prison for the murders, and that he escaped a number of times.

Another incident occurred on July 3, 1909. The *Crowley Signal* reported a fatal stabbing at a ball given by Aurelian Hebert in the community of Castille. Jack Melancon stabbed twenty-one-year-old Odulon Caruthers (Credeur) in the heart. Earlier records of Acadia Parish criminal dockets indicate that Jack Melancon was cited a number of times for such criminal activity as disturbing the peace by fighting, carrying a concealed weapon, being intoxicated, fighting and using loud obscene language in the presence of others on a public road.

According to Acadia Parish Docket No. 1711: "On Oct. 28, 1909, Leoval Meche did feloniously, willfully and maliciously shoot one, Ove Meche, with a pistol with intent to kill."

Betty Lyons Bourque, wife of Pat Bourque, is the daughter of Gadrac Arceneaux and Walker Lyons, one of the original settlers of the Marais Bouler area. Bourque related to me that most folks of the Marais Bouleur area were generally law abiding.

"It's just that the folks were very secluded, surrounded by vast marsh lands, without police, and so they took to settling their own disputes," Bourque explained. "It was rarely about stealing or other criminal intent."

According to Betty Bourque, her father's original tract of land was about five hundred acres, mostly swampland, purchased at a cost of about fifty cents per acre. Once, Walker Lyons was on the verge of losing his property but a family member from Crowley loaned him money to keep his land. Later, canals were dug to drain the swamp, creating farmland and so he planted cotton, sweet potatoes and corn.

Walker Lyons died in 1945, and his wife died later that year. Included in his obituary was a reference that said he was one of the original settlers of the Marais Bouler area.

NOTE: For a touch of true Cajun culture, visit the Marais Bouleur band performing "La Valse Criminelle" with Yvette Landry on bass, accordion and vocal; Blake Miller on accordion, bass, fiddle and vocal; Chris Segura on fiddle and vocal; Jacques Boudreaux on guitar and vocal; and Danny Devillier on drums. Also, former Louisiana poet laureate and former University of Louisiana at Lafayette professor of English Darrell Bourque wrote "Plainsongs of the Marais Bouleur: A Selection" in the March 5, 2004 issue of the *Journal of Popular Culture*.

CHAPTER 13

A BAD VIBE IN THE OLD FUNERAL HOME

THE OPELOUSAS MUSEUM AND INTERPRETIVE CENTER

Living history roams the Opelousas Museum and Interpretive Center, walking among the Clifton Chenier zydeco records and Civil War relics and around the barbershop chair where Clyde Barrow of Bonnie and Clyde fame got his last haircut. There are specters that refuse to leave the 1935 building, whose incarnations have included the Sibille's Funeral Home, a church and the Opelousas Library.

Director Delores Guillory had no idea of the building's history when she first started working at the Opelousas Museum. Her first clue came when she was alone in the building, sitting at her desk inside the office.

"The front door opened, and it closed," Guillory said. "I looked over and nobody came. I looked at the door, and there was no one."

Guillory even went so far as to check the outside porch and sidewalk, and both were empty. When her supervisor returned, she recalled the story. To her surprise, the supervisor laughed.

"That's when she told me about it once being a funeral home," Guillory said.

Other events followed, including hearing startling noises like something falling from the wall. Once a loud noise emanated from the Civil War room, and Guillory smelled cigarettes after investigating.

Another time, she was sitting in the hallway when the back door opened and closed. At first, she chalked it up to the security guard who liked to tease her about the ghosts, but when she called him up on the phone, he was at the park.

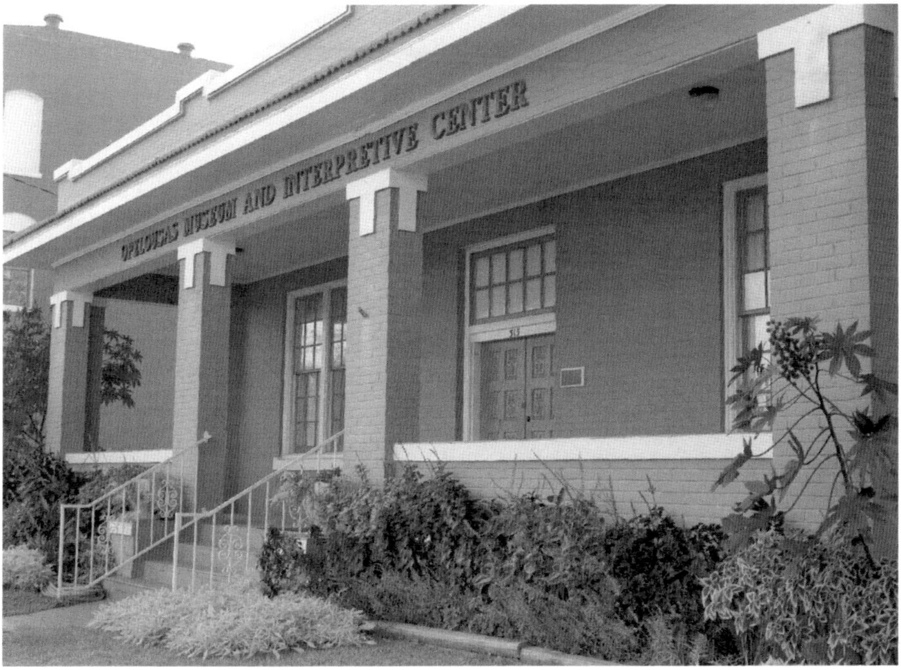

The Opelousas Museum and Interpretive Center has previously been Sibille's Funeral Home, a church and the Opelousas Library.

"I said okay, that was our ghost again."

Others have experienced sightings as well. One employee spotted something white and wispy moving across her line of sight by the Civil War Room.

"All of a sudden something went across cold cold, and she smelled perfume," Guillory explained. "We told her about the ghosts. The next day she quit."

A worker performing community service at the museum halted at the mannequin in the Mardi Gras display, a man bedecked in a long mink and velvet robe. The elaborate robe was created for Nolan Simmons, who reigned as King Orme XLVIII in the 1994 Carnival season in Opelousas. Today, the mannequin and elaborate custom are displayed inside a glass case, with a mirror behind so visitors can view all sides.

"She said I have to get out of here," Guillory related of the woman's experience at the mannequin. "She said there's a bad vibe in here."

Some people halt at the front door, feeling the paranormal vibe, and refuse to set foot inside, Guillory said.

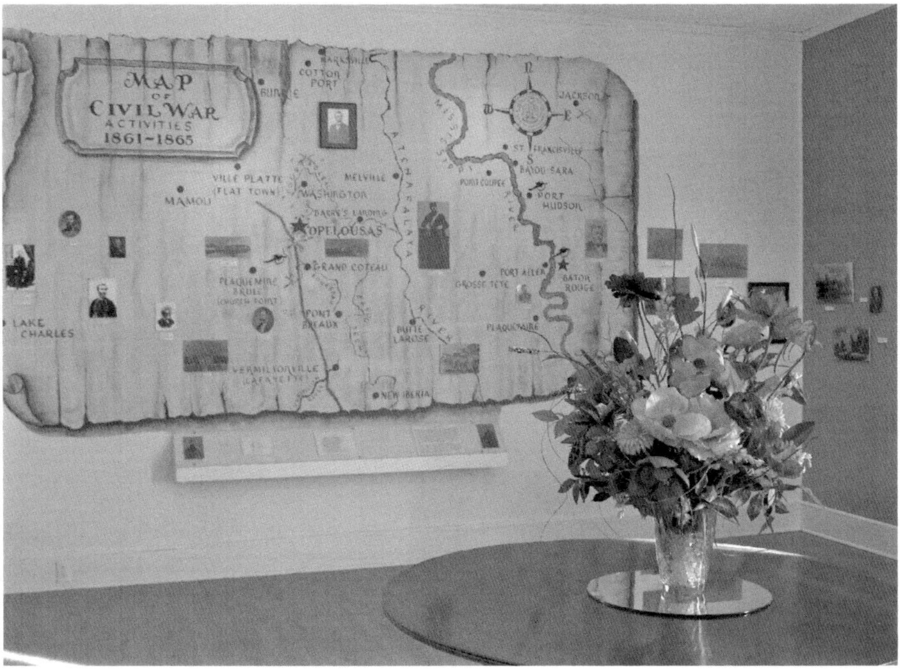

People have had paranormal experiences, such as hearing noises and smelling smoke, in the Civil War Room of the Opelousas Museum and Interpretive Center.

Louisiana Spirits paranormal investigators spent an evening in the museum and heard unusual sounds they couldn't account for, but they did debunk the mystery of the moving dolls in the display cases—dolls on display were known to be facing one way and then unexpectedly faced another. According to Jennifer Broussard of Louisiana Spirits, the dolls were not lying flat within the cases, so footsteps in the hall caused the cabinets to shake and move, thus causing the dolls to move as well. Investigator Charles Gardner managed to get one doll to turn completely around as he walked in the hallway, he said.

CHAPTER 14
THE FIRST SCARLETT O'HARA
CHRETIEN POINT PLANTATION

It's a long drive through rural roads to reach the elegant Chretien Point plantation just north of Lafayette outside the quaint town of Sunset in St. Landry Parish. Once you spot the stately home with its expansive yard and ancient live oak trees, it's hard to believe that Civil War bloodshed and dramatic pirate tales took place here. On top of all that, it's believed that photographer Jules Baguerry visited the plantation and sent photos of the home, including its dramatic staircase, to Hollywood producers for the film adaptation of the bestselling novel *Gone With the Wind*. Owners of the plantation have claimed the ramp knee staircase, as well as some of the home's history, was used in the 1939 award-winning film.

Chretien Point Plantation rests besides Bayou Bourbeaux, a waterway that allowed for cotton and other goods to be shipped throughout Louisiana. Hypolite Chretien Jr. built a twelve-room home here in 1835 for his wife, Felecité Neda, the daughter of a neighboring Spanish landowner. Some of the home's elegant features include great examples of plasterwork, finely carved woodwork, black Italian marble mantels and a dramatic staircase winding to the second floor.

When I was writing a ghost feature for the *Advocate* newspaper of Baton Rouge, a former owner, Louis Cornay, told me the tale most people know by heart in Acadiana, that Felecité Chretien killed a pirate on that famous staircase. Apparently, the Chretiens were friends of privateer Jean Lafitte, hero of the Battle of New Orleans, and the two gentlemen sold goods between them. Cornay related that one night, an aspiring pirate who knew of the Chretien family wealth tried to steal from Felecité. I've read other accounts that said the thieving pirate was not alone but with a group of marauders attempting to take over the premises after hearing Felecité was alone in the house.

Regardless, Felecité was a strong-willed woman who enjoyed playing cards, smoking cigars and riding horses astride. On the death of her husband from yellow fever, she took over management of the estate and became quite wealthy. She wasn't about to let anyone steal her belongings, let alone take over the house. Upon hearing of the pirate's entrance into the home, she crept down the stairs and promptly planted a bullet in the thieving man's head. Stumbling backwards down the stairs, the pirate's blood oozed forth and left stains on the eleventh step. The mark remaining on the plantation's staircase today is said to be evidence of this crime, and some people claim the scene in *Gone With the Wind* where Scarlett O'Hara shoots a thieving Union soldier on the staircase can be credited to Felecité's bravery.

In addition to the pirates and their escapades at Chretien Point, the plantation and neighboring bridge over Bayou Bourbeaux were scenes of intense Civil War action in 1863 (see chapter 21). Union major general Nathaniel P. Banks took over the house and everything inside and burned several outbuildings but saved the mansion. One story has it that Felecité's son, Hypolite Chretien III, was the reason Union soldiers spared the home after the crippled man struggled to the second-floor balcony and made a Masonic sign with shaking hands.

Herman de Bachellé Seebold tells another tale in his *Old Louisiana Plantation Homes and Family Trees*. According to Seebold, Felecité heard of the Yankees' arrival via a scouting slave and developed a plan of action. She had heard of a German countess who outsmarted Napoleon's army by greeting him with food and wine, so Felecité did the same. She met General Banks at the gate and invited him and his men to dine on elaborate tables filled with food and wine beneath the plantation's oak trees.

Banks agreed, enjoying the feast, and vowed to only search for Confederate soldiers within the house. After finding none, he proceeded to steal everything worth taking. But Felecité's kindness convinced him to spare the house.

In its heyday, Chretien Point included twelve thousand acres and five hundred slaves producing cotton. For many recent years, it served as a bed-and-breakfast and wedding site. Today, Chretien Point Plantation is a private residence surrounded by twenty acres.

THE GHOSTS OF CHRETIEN POINT

During his time living at Chretien Point, Cornay heard many odd sounds and believed the home contained several ghosts including men, women and children. He heard sounds of children playing in the parlor, a woman's soft footsteps walking across the floor and random children's laughter. Tour guides reported seeing chairs rocking on their own accord.

At first, Cornay was skeptical. But the more he mentioned out loud that there was no such thing as ghosts, the more he heard sounds that offered no explanation. The same happened with visitors who disputed the presence of paranormal activity. It was as if the ghosts were proving them wrong.

"The thing that really makes the difference is that if you respect that they are about, then there's no problem," Cornay told me for the *Advocate* interview. "If you don't acknowledge their existence, then things happen."

For instance, once when he joked about the existence of the staircase ghost, his car's horn went off in the middle of the night. Cornay stumbled outside in a sleepy blur and brushed his hand across the dashboard as if to knock away the invisible hand. The horn stopped blowing. Cornay returned to his bed and a deep sleep only to dream of smoke coming from the car's steering column. The next morning, smoke was pouring from the car but stopped when he moved his hand, once again, across the steering wheel.

Cornay believed that the pirate might have been the cause. "The ghost that has given us the most trouble is this pirate Felecité killed on the stairs that night."

Another time, a tourist visiting the plantation made fun of the ghosts' existences. Later that evening, the fire alarm sounded in the tourist's motel miles away—but only in his room.

Cornay and his wife once heard men talking in the back hall, but no one was there, at least no one visible. Later, a tourist arrived and said his great-grandfather, who served in the Union army, had taken a photo of three union officers standing at the foot of the staircase talking.

Cornay viewed the otherworldly residents as energy sources of those who lived there before.

"Maybe it's a little presumptuous of us that everything was created that we can see," he said.

Above all, he told me, once they are given respect, they offer respect in return.

"Our ghosts are not the scariest of ghosts," he related. "If you respect them, they respect you. We have to be good. Give everybody their space."

CHAPTER 15

CREOLE GHOSTS

JOHN LAFLEUR AND HISTORIC WASHINGTON

John LaFleur is on a roll these days. The seventh-generation descendant of both Louisiana Creoles and Acadians, he's mad that one culture has been superseded by another.

Mention "Creole" to a Louisiana resident and you're bound to hear several different definitions and start an argument. Some refer to Creoles, especially those in New Orleans, as first-born citizens of the colony of French and Spanish descent. Others believe the term defines those of mixed races. In South Louisiana, outside of the New Orleans city limits, Creole has been used in the mixed-race sense, even labeling the forerunner of zydeco music as "Creole" music.

"Creole simply means native born," LaFleur explained one day in his Creole cottage located in the historic town of Washington, about forty-five minutes north of Lafayette in St. Landry Parish. "And that applied to all of Louisiana."

The Merriam-Webster dictionary defines "Creole" as:

> *1) a person of European descent born especially in the West Indies or Spanish America;*
> *2) a white person descended from early French or Spanish settlers of the United States Gulf states and preserving their speech and culture;*
> *3) a person of mixed French or Spanish and black descent speaking a dialect of French or Spanish;*
> *4) a language evolved from pidginized French that is spoken by blacks in southern Louisiana.*

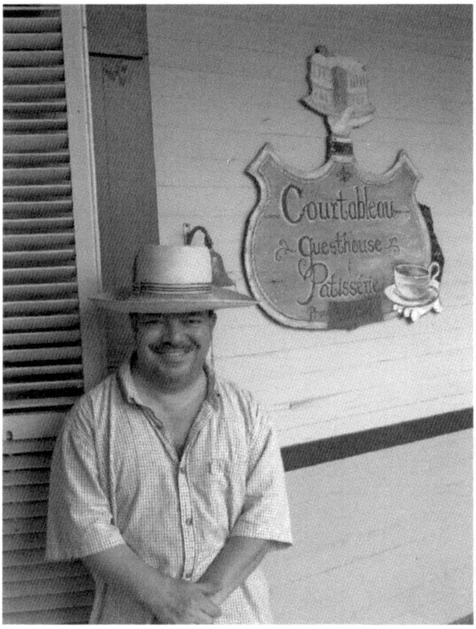

John LaFleur is descended from both Louisiana Creole and Acadian ancestors—and one of those relatives may be visiting him at his Washington home.

By applying all of these terms, most of the residents of South Louisiana are Creole, LaFleur insists, including those we now call "Cajun." Although the Acadians (Cajuns) originally settled the Maritime Provinces of present-day Canada, they were exiled by the British beginning in 1755 and made their way to Louisiana after years of living in exile. At the time, the Louisiana colony was helmed by Spain, which was Catholic, sympathetic and welcoming to the displaced Acadians. Because Cajuns were farmers, the Creole residents in Louisiana at the time were not as welcoming, and the Cajuns pretty much kept to themselves. When the Americans took over Louisiana, they heard the Cajuns referring to each other by their nickname, "Cadjin," which sounded like "Cod-gen" and the Americans began calling them Cajuns.

Due to their sometimes isolated and low economic status, the Cajuns weren't always treated well. In the last few decades, the culture has come into its own, with a Cajun Renaissance of music, culture and food.

Today, most of South Louisiana is known as Cajun Country, stretching up like a triangle to the middle of the state and reaching from the Mississippi State Line to the Texas border. In 1971, the Louisiana legislature deemed twenty-two parishes as "Acadiana," the region where Acadians/Cajuns settled, although most Louisiana residents refer to only the southwestern area around Lafayette as Acadiana.

LaFleur takes great exception to living in "Cajun Country," for the region consists of descendants of both Cajuns and Creoles. He has written about these cultural labels in his book, *Louisiana's French Creole Culinary & Linguistic Traditions: Facts vs. Fiction, Before and Since "Cajunization"* as well as his cookbook, *Creole Secrets of Louisiana: A Cultural Legacy*.

"The fact is, all Louisiana Creoles share the same French cultural base, to which is added other ethnic 'ingredients' of African, Amer-indian, Spanish, Italian and yes, German origin," LaFleur writes.

"My mission is to expose the truths of my culture," he said. "We're going to align history with reality."

Creole Cottage

A few years back LaFleur—a high school teacher, international interpreter and tour guide—had been looking for a new place to live. He was visiting a Washington graveyard for research when he spotted his current abode, a two-story house with a separate dining and kitchen area, louvered shutters, pitched roof and a staircase on the porch.

"Something about this house spoke to me," he said. "I said, 'This has to be a French Creole house.'"

As he walked over to the home, he spotted a "For Sale" sign in back. The prospect was enticing, but LaFleur was broke at the time and couldn't imagine a way to purchase the property.

"I got a call from people who wanted me to give them a tour of Europe and paid in Euros," he explained. "It was better than dollars. I barely land, and I get another call to do another tour! I suddenly had the money to buy this house and renovate."

It was as if someone was looking out for LaFleur. But that someone may have left the physical plane a long time ago.

After he closed on the Washington property, which LaFleur intended to renovate and turn into apartments, he came home to his Creole cottage and found an envelope under his door. Inside were documents listing the first owner as a Jean-Baptiste André dit la Fleur.

"I told myself I was losing my mind," he said of the coincidence between the names of the original owner and himself.

He asked a neighbor who worked at the St. Landry Parish Archives, and the neighbor concurred that his home was once part of the LaFleur Plantation.

He changed his mind about the apartment.

"I became interested in family culture and who we were," he said.

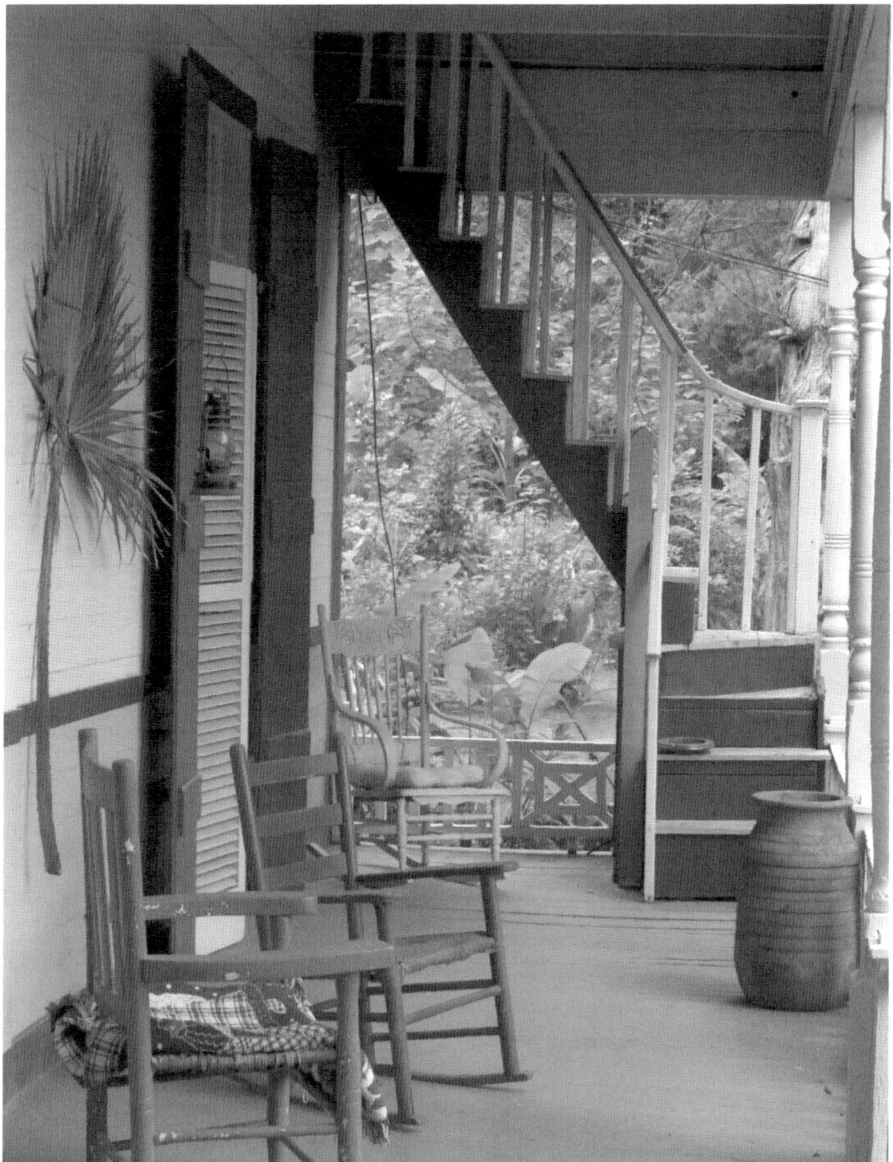

A mischievous woman haunts the LaFleur House in Washington.

FORMER CREOLE RESIDENTS

LaFleur was no stranger to ghosts. His former residence in nearby Grand Prairie had its share.

"I didn't believe in ghosts until I lived in that house," he said.

The first night LaFleur stayed in his Washington Creole cottage, he heard footsteps making their way down the hallway. He thought it was the carpenter, but that guest had been sleeping soundly. He didn't think too much of the incident and went about restoring the home's wooden beams and floors, adding authentic colors such as indigo and purchasing antiques typical of Louisiana Creole culture.

"This is a living Creole monument house," he insists of the registered historic property.

After living in the house for a year or two, LaFleur held a small party for guests. After the last guests had left, about 10:00 p.m., he heard knocking.

"I went into a cold shiver," he related. "Something said, 'Do not open the door.'"

He thought about calling the police, but curiosity about who was in his house with him made him look down the hallway. A woman dressed in a black mourning outfit stood before him, her face only an outline with dark eyes gazing at him. LaFleur yelled, and the woman turned and then flew out the door.

LaFleur searched the house but no one was there.

Later, when LaFleur discussed this with the Washington chief of police, he received a snide answer.

"He [the chief of police] said, 'Washington is full of ghosts. You don't know that?'" LaFleur related.

The police would hear from LaFleur again. He was awakened at 2:00 a.m. by people talking in the house. Since LaFleur was a teacher, he assumed it was kids from the high school hanging around, being mischievous. He wasn't scared—until he heard footsteps going up the stairs.

"And then it freaked me out," he said. "They were speaking in French!"

The next thing he knew, a face was hovering above his saying, "Get up! Get up!"

The chief of police arrived soon after LaFleur made a call. There were no cars on the street, and of course, no one else with warm blood running through his veins inside the house.

"He said it was ghosts, to get on your knees and pray," LaFleur recounted. "'If you know what's good for you, get on your knees and pray.' That's what he said."

LaFleur shared his experiences with his priest, who advised him to address the spirit in French and tell her that he was the owner now, and she needed to find rest. When he moved his bedroom upstairs, his experiences with the afterlife ceased.

OTHERWORLDY VISITORS

Because LaFleur uses the home as the Courtableau House Plantation Bed and Breakfast, guests have had their share of experiences with the apparition. Once when a writer had visited and was interviewing LaFleur, she asked about ghosts. Seconds later, a nearby chair "shook like an earthquake," LaFleur said.

Another guest staying in the downstairs bedroom saw a woman appear in her mirror.

"She said, 'She likes what you're doing,'" LaFleur related. "She said she was cantankerous before, but she won't be now."

Another guest, who was expecting a baby, felt someone touch her in the night. At first, she thought it was her husband, but then, she spotted a petite lady who vanished like a puff of smoke.

LaFleur's favorite story concerns a cantankerous woman who was very much alive, a high-maintenance bride who stayed at the bed-and-breakfast and complained about everything. LaFleur wasn't staying in the house that night and, at 2:00 a.m., received a phone call from the new husband who exclaimed that the bride was in his truck, demanding they leave. During the night, the bride had visited the bathroom only to find an angry old lady in her mirror who promptly reached out of the reflection and pulled her hair.

Who is the lady haunting LaFleur's Courtableau House Plantation Bed and Breakfast?

The original plantation owner had a free woman of color or slave whom he fell in love with after his wife had died. The two lived almost as husband and wife, LaFleur said. When the owner passed away, the man's children forbade the woman of color to attend the wake.

"Some say she's haunting the place because she's looking for her husband," LaFleur explained.

Creole Coincidences

Besides the occasional visit from the woman from beyond, LaFleur has experienced coincidental events dealing with his Creole cottage. Years before, his grandmother had tired of living without luxuries so she went to a Ville Platte furniture store and purchased a Julie Bock print of camellias, which she placed on her wall. One day something told LaFleur to go to the local flea market, and when he did, he thought of his grandmother. Looking up, he discovered a Julie Bock print for sale.

"When I thought of my grandmother, there was my grandmother's print!" he said.

LaFleur knew it was the actual print his grandmother had purchased because, as a child, he had fixed the frame with a tree branch and this print was exactly the same.

Once LaFleur was in need of furniture for his new abode but was not sure what he wanted. He decided to go shopping anyway.

"I just knew I had to go," he said.

He found a French walnut post daybed with the front piece sporting a wooden circle with a small inscription of *MA* carved into the wood. The week before he had taught a lesson on Marie Antoinette and was fascinated by her story. The summer before he was in Versailles. He's convinced this piece of furniture was the legendary queen's, before she lost her head.

Upon restoring the cottage, LaFleur drew up plans for balustrades. He knew exactly what he wanted to grace the front of the house. He was returning home from work one day, turned the corner at a Washington antique dealer and saw exactly enough cypress pieces to use for the job.

"And they were the perfect height to the exact design I had drawn," he said.

Washington a Ghost Town

The quaint town of Washington with its bed-and-breakfasts and antique shops a few miles north of Opelousas has more than its share of ghosts. The town dates back to 1770 when a Catholic church was built along Bayou Courtableau. Beginning in 1820, the town expanded due to the bayou's steamboat traffic and soon became a vital transportation hub for sugar, cotton, cattle and other products.

Much of Washington consists of original historic homes, warehouses and businesses, with several on the National Register of Historic Places. The bayou is no longer a transportation mecca, but the Steamboat Warehouse Restaurant allows visitors a peek into a bygone era, as it occupies one of the original bayou-side warehouses, built between 1819 and 1823.

It was at the Steamboat Restaurant that Louisiana Spirits captured one of its most dramatic paranormal experiences on tape (see chapter 6). The paranormal investigators were sitting by the restaurant's bar when they were convinced a live person was in the room with them. When the said person began coming toward them, they were scared for their safety, even pulling a tire iron off the wall in defense.

But no one was there.

Others have witnessed the bus cart, which was at a standstill, take on a life of its own and roll across the brick floor, as if someone had pushed it into motion. Some wait staff have felt invisible hands pushing them, and the owner claimed to have heard sounds of a busy restaurant around two in the morning—when the restaurant was deserted.

Outside on the bayou a young ghostly girl has been seen walking along its edge. Another time she was holding onto the hand of an older lady.

The most famous ghost story lies within the Nicholson Home, built in 1835 by the first mayor of Washington, Captain Gerand Carriere. During the Civil War, the home was used as a hospital, and bloodstains on the upstairs floor are testaments to that fact. The one-legged soldier who refuses to leave is another.

The amputated soldier appeared numerous times to the former owner Mildred Nicholson and her grandson, according to Christine Word's *Ghosts Along the Bayou: Tales of Hauntings in Southwestern Louisiana*. Visitors to the home received chilling pains in their legs and felt a need to leave, and Word herself developed a chill in her left arm that lasted for months. Her visit to the Nicholson home left a mark on her forever, she said.

"Although the chill was unwelcome at first, it soon become my personal battle scar," Word writes in *Ghosts Along the Bayou*. "In fact, it's as though I have been bestowed with some point of reference to detect a real haunting. Because now, when I enter a place where there is a soul at unrest, I can tell."

CHAPTER 16

THE CREATIVE VORTEX OF ARNAUDVILLE

Spiritual medium Allyson Glynn Schram was heading down Highway 31 toward her home in Arnaudville when she passed the Bethlehem Baptist Church Cemetery and "Spirit," which she calls those in another plane communicating with her, showed her two young African American girls wearing Sunday-go-to-meeting clothes and holding hands. Allyson immediately thought "sisters" and vowed to return to the cemetery because she was convinced the two girls resided in the identical tombs close to the front of the graveyard.

When she returned she discovered the tombs belonged to Beatrice Clark Taylor, 1907–1998, and Lou Ann Clark Taylor, 1913–1996.

"They came through standing here as the same age," Schram explained.

Schram imagines they might have lived together, hence being buried right next to each other in identical graves. Even the fake flowers adorning their stark white concrete tombs matched.

"I would think that [sisters being buried side by side] would be rare," she said. "Usually it's husband and wife."

The cemetery is located just outside Arnaudville on Highway 31 where it meets McVeigh Road. Vicky Cormier drives this stretch of highway on her way to work each morning, and routinely she's greeted by an African American man standing to the right of the graves by a cluster of trees in the small cemetery. He wears thin cotton pants and a cotton shirt that's slightly skewed, as if he's just returned from working in the fields. Cormier is convinced he's a farmer, but one who's tilled the soil in another time.

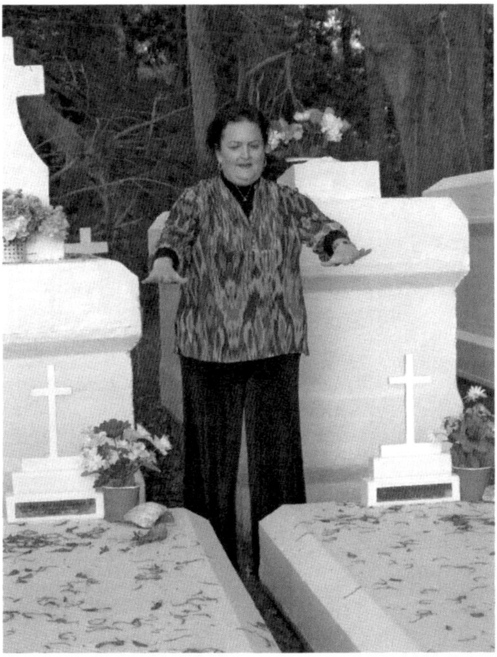

Spiritual medium Allyson Glynn Schram stands before the tombs of Beatrice Clark Taylor and Lou Ann Clark Taylor in the Bethlehem Baptist Church Cemetery of Arnaudville.

"He's standing there, like he's waiting for me," she said. "He just kind of stands there. It's almost like he just wants to be noticed."

Like Schram, Cormier is a sensitive, and she senses more than actually sees the man in the cemetery. The way she describes it, he's visible through her peripheral vision but not if she turns her head and looks at him straight on. In her mind, she's convinced he was a poor slave or sharecropper and spoke French and perhaps a little English.

"He was definitely not a man of means, and I can guarantee if he had an education, it was very little," Cormier said.

When the time change occurs in late October, her drive to work is too dark to make out the cemetery, so Cormier's farmer disappears until spring. But even in Daylight Savings Time, the farmer will not show up for long periods of time.

What he's trying to impart to Cormier, she doesn't know.

"I don't understand why he shows up and why he doesn't," she said.

It makes perfect sense for the farmer to reach out to Cormier, however. Cormier leads classes in metaphysics in the backroom of her home in Arnaudville, everything from a weekly Intuitive Development Circle to crystal skull gatherings. At her weekly circles, she and participants accept messages from the beyond to bring healing and comfort for attendees.

It wasn't always this way, she said. Although she can't remember in her youth having a particular gift in communicating with those who had passed on, she almost died as a child, and that experience transformed her life. At seven months old, her heart wasn't working properly so she routinely cried without making a sound and barely ate. Her frightened parents took her to Charity Hospital in New Orleans while family and friends back in Acadiana prayed for her recovery. Cormier needed immediate heart surgery, and the doctor able to perform the procedure only visited Charity once a month. On the Monday after Easter, they were told that if they didn't do the surgery that week, they would have to wait another month and she might not survive. Dr. Michael Debakey, a renowned cardiac surgeon, happened to make a visit at the same time and performed the surgery that saved her life.

When she woke up from surgery, Cormier explained, her parents heard her screaming from the hallway. Afterward, while they waited for her to recover, her father unwrapped a baloney sandwich, and the paper made a crinkling noise, causing Cormier to laugh.

"Dad said he had never heard me laugh out loud," she recalled.

Growing up, Cormier didn't find herself talking to dead people like the child in *The Sixth Sense*, outside of being scared at things she sensed at night. She grew up in a Catholic household and was part of the Charismatic Renewal Movement while in her thirties. One night at a prayer circle, the priest, Father Nunez, told her she had a gift of prophecy, a comment that would remain with her for years.

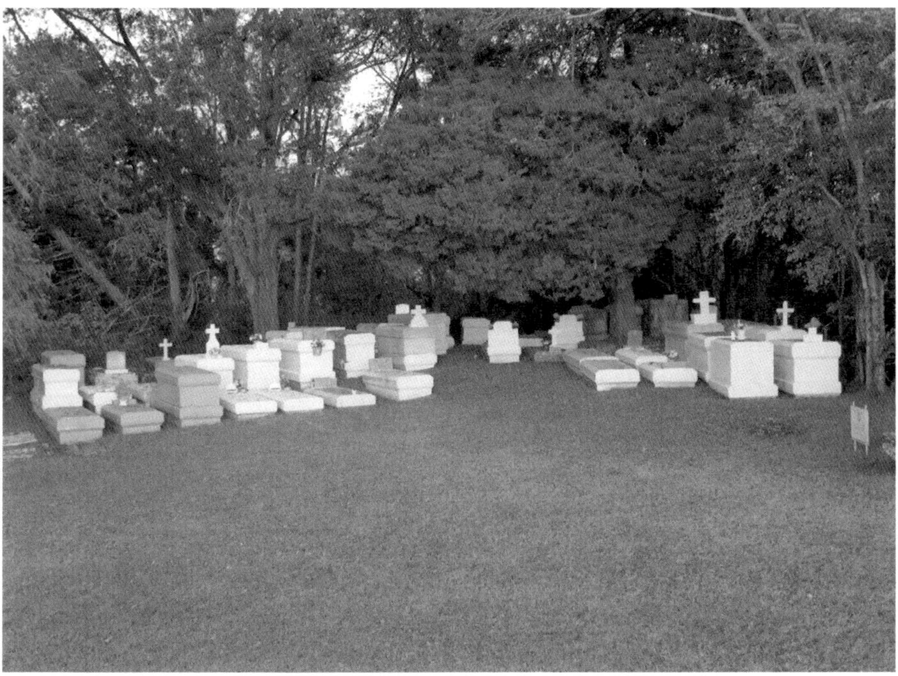

The ghost of a farmer has been seen at the Bethlehem Baptist Church Cemetery of Arnaudville.

Time went by and Cormier met Becca Begnaud, a South Louisiana traiteur and healer (see chapter 5) who invited her to attend intuitive classes in Baton Rouge. At first, Cormier attended classes sporadically and then regularly. When she bought a house in Arnaudville in 2010, she and Begnaud led classes in her backroom, a comfortable space with items gracing the wall that represents Cormier's background, from *The Last Supper* to her collection of crystals. Today, Cormier leads classes weekly and brings in special speakers on occasion.

During her educational phase, Cormier said she struggled with trying to balance New Age thought with Catholicism. Through it all, however, she remembered the words of Father Nunez.

"What is this but the gift of prophecy?" she asked of her ability.

No Coincidences

Psychotherapist Carl Jung believed that humans share a collective unconscious and that no meaningful coincidences are accidental. He called it synchronicity.

About the time Cormier was considering a move to Arnaudville, Schram and her husband, Charlie, were living in Lafayette. They loved their urban condo in the tony development known as River Ranch, but Schram had cut out a photo of an older home and placed it in a vision book, thinking that eventually she would return to that kind of lifestyle.

Wanting to meet another medium, Schram connected Cormier by phone.

"When I moved to Lafayette, I wanted to meet like-minded people," Schram said. "Spirit told me to call Vicky."

Schram and Cormier met for pizza when Cormier was in the process of buying a new home. After Cormier purchased her Arnaudville house, Schram and her husband stopped by with a house-warming gift.

"We had no idea where Arnaudville was," she said with a laugh.

The meeting was preceded by an unusual message from Spirit.

"That morning when I got up and went to the kitchen to make coffee Spirit said to me, 'I am eighty-eight,'' Schram recalled. "I asked Charlie if his parents were eighty-eight when they passed, and he said, 'No.'"

Later, when the three were enjoying an afternoon on Cormier's Arnaudville patio, Schram asked Cormier if eighty-eight meant anything to her and she said, "No," as well.

As the afternoon progressed, Cormier mentioned that the house next door was up for sale since the owner had recently died. It appeared that family members were at the house at the time, so Charlie Schram went next door to investigate.

When he returned, he recounted that he had met with the former owner's children and toured the house.

And by the way, the owner had died at age eighty-eight.

"Our eyes all popped open," Schram explained. "I said, 'Maybe we need to go look at that house.'"

As soon as she entered the home next-door, Schram felt Spirit and did something she hardly ever does—told the family members she was psychic.

"But they welcomed us in and took us around the house," Schram said.

Still, they couldn't believe they would actually leave Lafayette.

"We left Arnaudville and thought, 'Dear God, it's like driving to Baltimore, it's so far away,'" Schram recalled with a laugh.

Then Charlie Schram was offered a job in Breaux Bridge, a neighboring town to Arnaudville.

"About a month or so later they bought the house and moved next door," Cormier explained. "It really happened quickly."

Both Cormier and Schram, now next-door neighbors, offer psychic readings to the public and both believe that communication remains between the living and the dead.

"Even those who have gone into Spirit and are now with God can stay connected to the people they love within the vibration of love," Schram told me. "That's when a medium like I am can validate with what they're saying, to give comfort and peace and to let you know they are still around."

Ironically, both Cormier and Schram report feelings of those who have passed on within their homes, neither of which is frightening. Cormier smells smoke in her house on occasion and believes it to be from Mr. Ackal, the former owner who died of emphysema and who was a smoker. Cormier sleeps in the bedroom once used by Mrs. Ackal and will smell smoke at the end of the bed.

"I know he's there," she said. "When I moved in he was there. But I have no idea what connection that is."

Schram believes the former owners still linger in her house along with "T.J.," one of the seven children raised in the home who died when he was seventeen. Schram has seen a male teen, tall and thin in straight-leg jeans and a white T-shirt walking barefoot throughout the house. When young women visit, activity attributed to T.J. increases.

"He especially loves pretty young women," Schram said.

The mother, whom Schram calls Miss Anna, was a sweet woman in life and a traiteur, or Cajun healer. Schram believes Miss Anna wanted her to buy her home. Since moving in, Schram has found Miss Anna's prayer cards and a few other items.

"I was on my laptop early one day, and I heard a sweet female voice saying, 'Pushing buttons,' and I knew it was her," she said.

ARNAUDVILLE APPARITIONS

Arnaudville sits along the confluence of bayous Fuselier and Teche, east of Grand Coteau and north of Breaux Bridge and Cecila, a strategic intersection that gave the town its first name, *Le Juncture*. The heart of town winds through both bayous, with old-fashioned storefronts sporting businesses such as Tom's Fiddle and Bow, a locally owned grocery store, the craft brewery Bayou Teche Brewing and bed-and-breakfasts. Renowned Louisiana artist George Marks returned to his hometown of Arnaudville about ten years ago to take care of his parents and stayed, building up a vibrant arts scene that includes the NuNu Arts and Culture Collective, the Frederick l'Ecole Des Arts school, the annual Fire & Water celebration in winter and 2013's *La Semaine Francais*, a week of France-Louisiana collaboration. Because of Marks's work, Arnaudville is considered the Deux Bayous Cultural District.

"Arnaudville pulls creative, metaphysical and spiritual energy to this area," Schram said, attributing this to the bedrock makeup or the prayers of its Catholic residents, including the neighboring Jesuit Center in Grand Coteau. "Arnaudville and this land are conducive to activity. There is a reason that this land holds the energy and the energy imprint."

One of the town's newest businesses is the Little Big Cup coffeeshop. Located in the center of Arnaudville, this delightful and historic spot is great for enjoying an authentic South Louisiana meal, a cup of coffee and great conversation with town natives, many of whom still speak French.

And maybe there's a customer or two who hangs around unseen.

Cormier and Schram visited one day, peering into the dining room space renovated from an old warehouse. Schram instantly felt energy emanating from a boxed space at the end of the counter toward the back of the room. She asked the owners what used to exist there, if anything, and was told that area was a small room where two brothers lived.

And interestingly enough, they both died there.

Journalist Floyd Knott, who wrote historical features for the *Teche News*, delved into the history of the Widow Alexis Mayer House, one of the oldest homes in Arnaudville. He sought the help of researcher David Lanclos and discovered that the house was built in 1828. When Lanclos and Knott attended a local genealogy meeting, they unearthed even more.

"Family lore was that Madame Mayer so loved her yard that her ghost still roams outside the house," he wrote in his *Les Vieux Temps* column in 2008.

Lanclos took photos of the house and the property's oak trees only to find what looked like a ghost within the bark of the tree. Knott and others have repeated the task, finding a woman clad in "a sun bonnet, shawl, dress and shoes…sitting on a branch facing the road.

"From stories about the widow Alexis Mayer, the image would likely be her," he concluded.

When Arnaudville resident Brenda Foytlin's father was alive and in his later years, he had no teeth. He used to joke around with Foytlin's kids by biting them. One day Brenda's three-year-old granddaughter ran to her exclaiming that the "old man had bit her arm." When Foytlin asked who the old man was, her granddaughter pointed to the recliner, making a face.

"It was the same face our father used to make when he was alive," Foytlin said.

Foytlin's father had died in the apartment behind their house. After he had passed away, they rented the apartment. Within a month, the tenant reported seeing a full-body apparition. Foytlin showed the tenant a photo of her father, and the tenant identified it as the ghostly image he had seen in the apartment.

Foytlin's father loved the kitchen and was a clean freak, she said. After his passing, her dog refused to go in the kitchen. Her dad didn't believe in dogs in the house.

CHAPTER 17

THE RAIN TREE OF BAYOU PORTAGE

You have to know where you're going to reach Bayou Portage and the spot where an ancient tree of a remarkable legend once stood. It's a placid stretch of bayou, a place where the road ends and a gentle slope allows for boats to enter into the murky waters. Along the banks, a houseboat is tied up, and nearby are remnants of watercraft that has seen better days.

If you look closely, you will spot the Indian mound on a neighboring property. The ancient mound is not accessible to the public, although many people have traveled to this quiet, remote spot to see both the mound and the mysterious Rain Tree that grew along the banks of Bayou Portage.

It all dates back to a story passed down among the Chitamachas. The natives who once lived along the bayou banks told of a fair-skinned man who appeared to the tribe speaking their language and owning extensive knowledge of many things. He taught them new ways to fish and grow crops and which foods to substitute for those not in season. One day, he told the tribe it was time for him to leave and do "his father's work," recalled Emile Stouff, a Chitimacha chief in *Chitimacha Notebook*. He found a cypress tree by the bayou's edge and climbed to the top.

"Then he told the Chitimachas, 'Whenever you need rain for your crops, come and wet this tree, and it will rain according to your needs,'" Stouff wrote. "That is how the Indians were blessed by the Great Spirit."

I had heard this legend in my years of researching ghost stories for newspapers in South Louisiana but had never found anyone to substantiate it nor tell of its whereabouts, until I met Allen Babineaux, a retired New

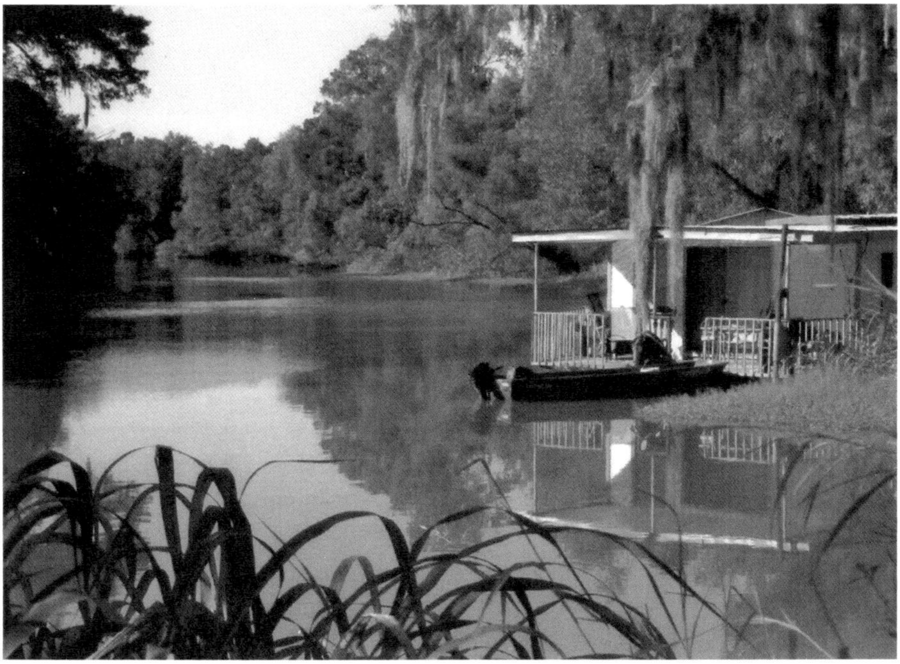

The legendary rain tree of the Chitimachas once stood on the banks on Bayou Portage, east of Loreauville.

Iberia fire chief. Babineaux's mother-in-law lived on Bayou Portage east of Loreauville, about forty-five minutes from Lafayette, on a piece of property that also included Indian mounds. She had related to Babineaux the story of the rain tree, adding that in her youth, during a bad period of drought, area farmers had hired a man to pray at the tree to bring rain. When they asked the hired man to join them for a cup of coffee, he declined and hurried away, saying it was about to storm.

"It rained so hard it flooded," Babineaux told me by phone from Sarasota, Florida, when I called to interview him for a 1997 story for the Baton Rouge *Advocate* newspaper.

During a more recent drought, when Babineaux lived in South Louisiana, he decided to try the tree out for himself.

"So the first time I go by the tree and ask for rain after a dry period, it rained!" he recalled at the 1990 Festivals Acadiens in Lafayette, recorded in *Swapping Stories: Folktales from Louisiana*. "I said, 'Oh well, that's just one of those things.' I'm not superstitious."

But he did it again.

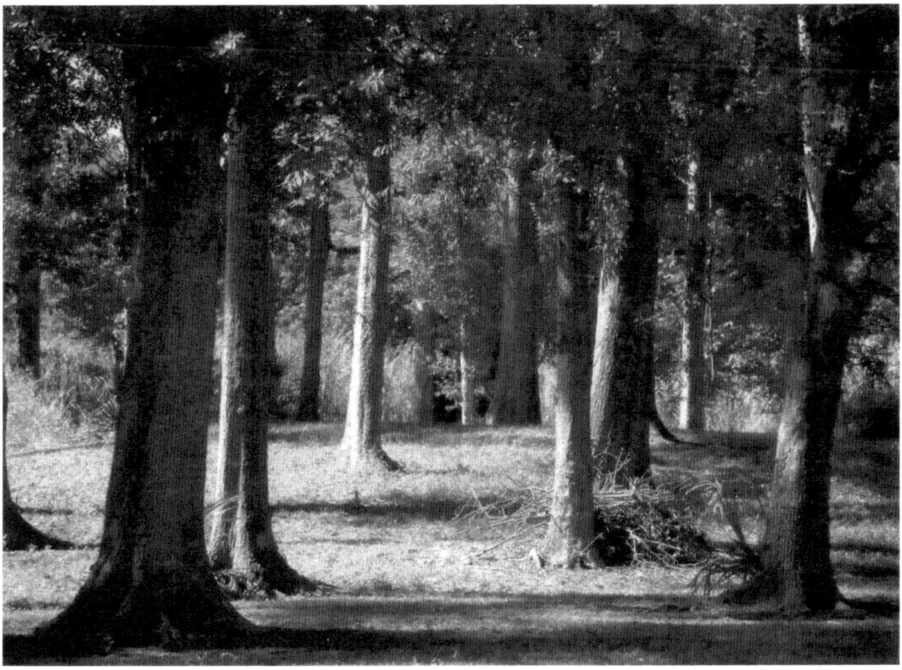

On the banks of Bayou Portage and the surrounding area lie many Native American mounds.

"Well, sometime later, the same thing happened," he recalled in *Swapping Stories*. "There was a dry period, I happen to be fishing, I noticed the water's way down. We needed rain. Cane farmers sorely need it. I said, 'I'm going to do this again, just to see what happened.'"

Babineaux sprinkled water on to the tree and asked for rain.

"And it rained before I got to the landing, which was 150 feet away," he said.

Babineaux tried it again and again. In total, Babineaux asked the tree for rain six times and six times it rained.

"It really happened six times in a row," he told me.

Alvin "Pem" Broussard, a Louisiana native with Native American and European ancestry, remembers the rain tree well. He lives near Bayou Portage, calls the waterway "T-Bayou" and believes, as do many of the Native Americans of the area, that the ancient cypress tree delivered rain when needed until it succumbed to old age and toppled into the bayou.

Broussard was born in a French-speaking Catholic home. He's still a practicing Catholic, but he's studied other religions, including that of his

Native American ancestry. He is a member of the Ishak Metis of the Sunrise Group, part of what historians have called the Attakapas tribe.

Broussard has been creating rain sticks in honor of the sacred tree that once grew along the bank of Portage Bayou. At first, he used bamboo, adding native inscriptions, directional markings, animal drawings and minute amounts of mud from the bayou where the tree once stood. Now, his rain sticks are created out of cypress wood, more aligned with the original tree, he said.

"The rain sticks," Broussard explained to me when I interviewed him for a story in *Country Roads* magazine of Baton Rouge, "they tie in with the sacred tree."

Does it still rain sans the sacred tree? Babineaux believes it still works.

"The last time that rain was asked for, the tree was actually down and lying on the bank," he recalled in *Swapping Stories*. "And it rained. So there are a lot of theories about this, but I seem to think that, maybe, there's a pipeline from that tree area all the way to the good Lord."

CHAPTER 18

A MISCHIEVOUS CHILD

THE GHOST OF NASH'S RESTAURANT

Nash's Restaurant in Broussard serves up fine Creole dishes, whether inside the elegant Victorian home or on the enclosed veranda that skirts the entire front of the house. It was the perfect lunch spot for a mini family reunion when my sister visited and my niece celebrated a birthday, so along with my mother and me, we made a lively foursome. And because the beautiful old home is, well, old, we decided to inquire if there were any family members lingering behind.

Our waitress smiled knowingly. She's had a few experiences, she said, and so have other members of the staff. Mostly waitresses hear their names being called or items moving about unexpectedly. In the women's bathroom once, our waitress witnessed the hand dryer turning on twice without cause.

The activity is playful and harmless, she insisted, like that of a precocious child. It could be that of young Edmond Comeaux.

The Victorian-style house with a wraparound porch and an onion-shaped cupola was built around 1908 for Edmond Joseph Comeaux and his wife, Cecile Lena St. Julien. Inside is a gracious staircase leading to the second floor, fireplaces and an exquisite bar area. Comeaux operated a mercantile in town and served as postmaster of Broussard. The couple had one child, Walter St. Julien Comeaux, who married Carmen Emilie Labbe. Walter Comeaux and his wife had eight children, one of whom was Edmund Joseph Comeaux II.

The restaurant is currently owned by Nash Barreca, a third-generation restaurateur from New Orleans. According to "The Haunted Table" by

Simonette Berry in the October 2011 issue of *Our Louisiana* magazine, his wife, Jenny, chalked up the paranormal activity in the restaurant to the mischievous child "Edmond."

"He died in the home of a fever when he was only four, according to his brother Mr. Walter, the previous owner," Berry writes.

Jenny Barreca has witnessed chairs moving and glass breaking of their own accord and the sounds of a child running up and down the hallway laughing, according to the article.

"Both customers and wait staff have encountered him, and a few have even seen him," she is quoted as saying.

Visitors to Nash's Restaurant can catch a firm glimpse of the boy—his portrait hangs in the hallway.

CHAPTER 19
THE CURSE OF ST. MARTINVILLE

THE BIENVENUE AND DUCHAMP HOMES

The small town of St. Martinville rests along Bayou Teche, far from the traffic of Interstate 10, the bustle of Lafayette and the problems that plague most cities. In its heyday, however, St. Martinville was a hub of activity, boasting of elaborate homes, hotels, theaters and an opera house. Settlers—from exiled Acadians to French royalists fleeing the French Revolution—were drawn to the area for its rich soil, developing plantations that made them rich. Charles Durand became so prosperous that he planted spiders in treetops and decorated the webs with gold and silver dustings for his daughter's wedding.

For obvious reasons, they nicknamed the town "le Petit Paris."

Today, St. Martinville attracts tourists who come to view Acadian history and the legend of Evangeline (see chapter 22), but the town has seen better days. Its downward spiral could be due to a curse delivered by a man who was wrongly accused and executed years before.

In the early morning of August 12, 1891, a thief used a ladder to scale the two-story Robertson home located on Main Street in St. Martinville, near the railroad tracks. The Robertson family had moved to South Louisiana from Illinois after J.S. Robertson was hired to work on the railroad. On the dark morning of August 12, the widow Mary Robertson was sleeping soundly when the thief arrived, entering her bedroom through her window. The thief tore her mosquito bar to pieces, cut her throat and then ransacked bookcases and other furniture looking for items of value. The widow's young daughter Belle apparently heard her mother cry and came to investigate.

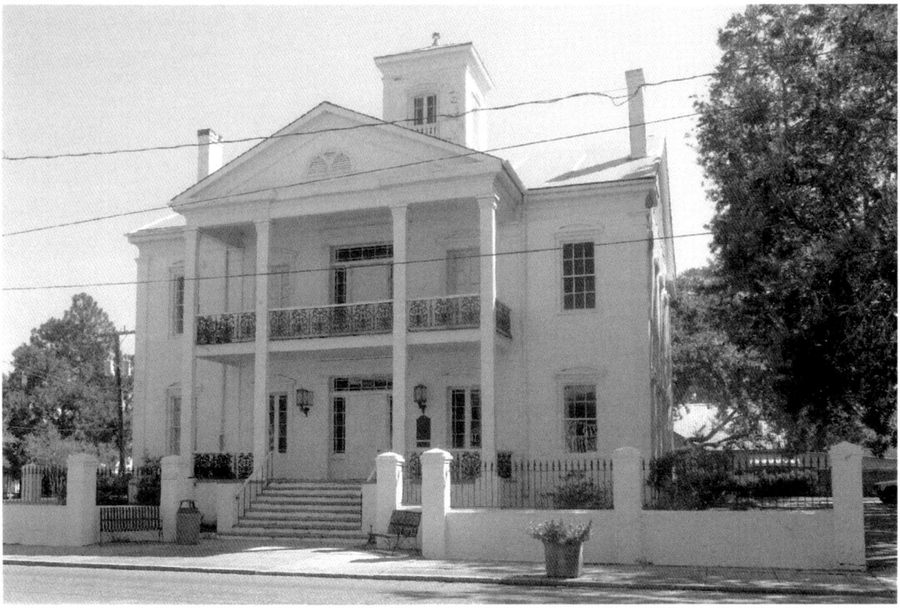

A ghostly woman has been seen standing at the window of the Duchamp House in St. Martinville.

She, too, was murdered. Another daughter, an invalid, survived and was later sent to live with relatives.

The mother-and-daughter murder shocked the community and crowds of St. Martinville citizens demanded justice. Several African Americans were arrested, but Louis Michel was the prime suspect. Michel had been a politician during the Republican Reconstruction period and was not liked by prominent white members of St. Martinville.

"Suspicion was strong against Louis Michel, as he had always had a bad reputation," reported the *Times-Picayune* newspaper of New Orleans.

Michel and Boy Chambers, who was a yard boy at the Robertson's home, were convicted of killing Belle Robertson and sentenced to life at the State Penitentiary in Baton Rouge. In the trial of Mary Robertson, both were found guilty and ordered to be hanged, even though testimony was contradictory and circumstantial. When Michel was asked if he could admit to some aspect of the murders that would save Chambers from hanging, he answered that "he could not because, being innocent, he knew nothing of either of the killings," reported the *Weekly Messenger* newspaper.

On March 24, 1893, Louis Michel enjoyed a bath, ate a full breakfast and received communion from his priest. He was then led to the scaffold, laughing and joking to the massive crowd assembled. He asked for wine and received it, and then he insisted he was being hanged for an old grudge and not for the Robertson's murders, of which he was innocent.

"Gentlemen, I know there are a great many of you who are anxious to see me die in the way in which I am to die today, but I am a man and I intend to die like a man," the *Times-Picayune* reported. "If I am on the gallows it is owing to grudges which many have had against me in my past political life. As to the crime of which I am accused, I am innocent and have a clear conscience to meet my master."

The *Lafayette Advertiser* reported:

> *Upon the scaffold Louis Michel was very calm and collected. After the reading of the death warrant by the sheriff, he was asked if he desired to make any statement. Michel advanced a step and addressing the captain of the regulators who was present, said, "You remember the night you and your men met and resolved to hang me or drive me from the parish? Well, I was under the house when you held the meeting. When you came to tell me to leave the parish, if you had tried to harm or hang me then, I would certainly have killed three or four of you with my Winchester, as I feared no man, being innocent."*

As the time of execution drew near, Michel's mood darkened. Before the noose slipped over his neck, he cursed the people of St. Martinville and the town itself, claiming that grass would grow in the street and nothing prosperous would happen from that moment forward.

Because of his height, Michel's feet touched ground when the scaffold opened. Michel managed to stay alive propped on his toes. The executioner quickly placed a board under Michel's feet and then whistled while he dug a hole. When the executioner considered the hole deep enough, he kicked the board away and the crowd watched as Michel was slowly strangled to death.

Later that spring, a newsboy noticed a St. Martinville man in a Houston railroad depot, a man who had disappeared from town immediately following the Robertson murders. The boy alerted the sheriff, and Paul Cormier was taken into custody. What happened next is unclear. Newspaper accounts in 1911 announced that Paul Brascourt (a possible Paul Cormier alias) had been picked up in Oklahoma for the Robertson murders and the killing of a Jewish merchant. He was acquitted on October 19, 1911, when a jury failed to find evidence that he was the missing Paul Cormier.

LA MAISON BIENVENUE

The Robertson home was built circa 1830 and is listed on the National Register of Historic Places. The two-story residence was originally the Bonin House, but it later housed the Bienvenue family and has since been referred to as the Bienvenue House. Today, it serves as a bed-and-breakfast.

Mary and Belle Robertson might still be living at the Bienvenue House. People who have stayed at the historic home have reported the ringing of a bell, lights going on and off and items being moved about in Belle's room.

Leslie Leonpacher, a former owner of the bed-and-breakfast, didn't know about the house's paranormal activity until her neighbor informed her of the murders. At first, the thought of sleeping in her new establishment terrorized her.

"The first night I played 'Phantom of the Opera,'" she related with a laugh. "Then I realized why? It was not in the least scary."

Leonpacher, an artist and author who now lives in Lafayette, never witnessed an apparition, but friends reported activity. One friend was sitting on the porch rocking chair with her eighteen-month-old baby on her lap.

"Her little baby sat up and started waving at one of the windows as if someone was there," Leonpacher said.

A client who routinely slept at the bed-and-breakfast opened a bottle of water, and the bottle cap rolled off the table into a corner. The next morning the cap was sitting on the table.

"He was really freaked out about it," said Leonpacher.

A local traiteur visited one day, walked into the house and announced that the place was haunted.

"She walked in and said there's a presence in this house, and it's very, very friendly," Leonpacher related.

Louisiana Spirits paranormal investigators spent the night at the Bienvenue House and experienced unusual EVPs. The sound of a woman's voice saying, "Gette pas"—or, "Don't look" in French—was captured on tape. When one investigator asked another if they were ready to go downstairs, a voice not belonging to either answered, "No."

Members of the Bienvenue family who lived in the house for years aren't as keen to calling the old homestead haunted. In fact, Dr. Willie Bienvenue, who lived in the house as a child and later for twenty-eight years as an adult, never had a paranormal experience. Neither did his parents.

"We never had a single unusual sound," Bienvenue said.

LA MAISON DUCHAMP

Years ago, I did a story on a Smithsonian exhibit at the old Duchamp House in St. Martinville, a building constructed as a classical revival mansion for David Sanchoz's daughter, Marie Amélie, and her husband, Eugene Auguste Duchamp de Chastaignier. The 1876 building had been used as a mercantile, the town's high school when the school burned down and, finally, the St. Martinville post office. According to an old article in the New Orleans *Times-Picayune*, which credited the Louisiana Tourist Commission, the building was the only home in the country converted into a post office. Another article states that the government did something unprecedented in obtaining the mansion—it honored the original architecture of the building, restoring the majestic home but converting the interior to align with postal needs, such as installing air conditioning. Among the post office's additions was a portrait of Henry Wadsworth Longfellow's beloved character Evangeline, from his epic poem of the same name, sitting on the banks of the Bayou Teche, waiting for her lover, Gabriel.

On the day I visited, I got a sneak peek inside the old building, built to resemble Duchamp's plantation in the West Indies. But Le Maison Duchamp is all Louisiana, created from the state's red cypress trees and red clay bricks pulled from Bayou Teche. The ironworks were shipped in from New Orleans, and a square cupola on the roof allowed residents a view of the town and their slaves on the nearby plantation.

The traveling Smithsonian exhibit I was there to enjoy took up the second floor of the building and the ample windows surrounding the space provided a fabulous view of the historic town. And because I'm a history buff, I spent an equal amount of time relishing the creaky wooden floors, the nineteenth-century architectural designs and portraits on the walls. On a lark, I inquired about the former owners and whether they were still around. My companion that day hinted that perhaps they were.

I never thought more on the building until an old friend who wishes to remain anonymous related a story. She was driving down Main Street through St. Martinville when she passed the old post office. The building sits on a corner where a traffic light is located, so my friend was paused in her car, waiting for the light to turn green.

She gazed up to a second-story window facing the historic church square and spotted a young woman in period dress staring out.

My friend was doing contract work in New Iberia, and she mentioned the odd experience when she arrived at her place of business. Co-workers said they knew about this woman and had heard the tales. One insisted that the woman was at the Duchamp house with a group of men at a business meeting. The woman became irritated with the group and moved to the window and stared out. She wasn't involved in the business, but what they had said had upset her, or so the story goes.

"When I saw her, I had a sense there was a group I couldn't see away from the window," my friend said.

One might assume the ghost is that of Marie Amélie, angry with her husband, who once served as mayor of St. Martinville, and the group of men could be attributed as civic leaders. Monsieur Duchamp also served as president of the St. Martin Parish Police Jury for thirty years, so it's likely many meetings took place in the home.

There's also a tragic side to the tale. Between 1880 and 1884, Monsieur Duchamp lost $75,000 of the family fortune, some say to gambling. Perhaps the group of men were bankers, or worse.

After losing his fortune, Duchamp sold the building to merchant Husville P. Fournet. Duchamp died in 1898 and was buried at St. Martin de Tours Catholic Church Cemetery on the square. Fournet's heirs later sold the building to the U.S. government for use as a post office.

Madame Duchamp died at her residence on Thursday, May 15, 1913, at the age of seventy-one. According to her obituary, "She was the mother of the members of the firm of Duchamp Hardware Company." The building was posted to the National Register of Historic Places on April 5, 1972.

CHAPTER 20
JUST TRAVELING THROUGH

THE GHOSTS OF MILTON CROSSING

Within Lafayette Parish but only a heartbeat away from the city of Lafayette lies the sleepy town of Milton. The small town hugs the Vermilion River and is a collection of small businesses, farms and residences. It's hard to imagine today that Milton was once a bustling operation, with sugar cane and other products moving up and down the river by steamboat.

One of the first-recorded residents of the Milton area was an Attakapas Indian named Bernard, son of Ashnoya. Explorers and trappers followed, and cattle ranchers and farmers came soon after. But what was needed most was a way to cross the Vermilion River. Milton became the location of a river ferry.

Early Cajun residents acquiring land through Spanish land grants (Spain owned the Louisiana colony at the time) included Joseph Broussard dit Beausoleil, an Acadian hero; Pierre Vincent; Joseph Boudreaux; Anselm Thibodeaux; Jean-Baptiste Guillaume Montet; and Jean-Baptiste Trahan. Thibodeaux settled on the east bank of the river near a coulee, and Montet fenced two hundred acres and set up a cotton gin and blacksmith shop. Odilion Broussard operated a mercantile store and a two-story home on the river's west side.

As early as the 1820s, a ferry is mentioned in the Milton area. In the 1880s, a bridge was constructed across the Vermilion River, with the current structure built in 1948.

The town that grew around this transportation hub was later named for Dr. Milton R. Cushman, who practiced medicine in the area and served as the town's first postmaster.

Lynwood Vincent grew up alongside the Vermilion River on land that stretches back in his family to the Spanish land grant. Born in 1919, Vincent remembers when neighbors would bring their milk to the cold spring on his property, nature's own refrigerator. He recalls sugar cane being moved down the river by steamboat when the cane syrup factory was operating in town.

And he remembers the disembodied voices that would visit on occasion.

As a younger man he was walking home with friends one day and left them by the coulee at the edge of his property. As he passed an old oak tree, he felt and heard two men walking behind him, as if they were carrying on a conversation and walking by. The hairs on his head stood straight up, he said. Another time, he heard a male sigh behind him.

At times, Vincent hears unexplained voices outside the home. When he looks, he can see clear across the field, but no one is there.

Vincent served as a French translator in World War II, helping to liberate France during the Norman invasion and POWs in Germany. A wall in his home sports the many medals he acquired during the war, and he'll proudly show off his letter from French president Charles de Gaulle.

Even though the paranormal activity that has existed on his property is pretty odd, Vincent shrugs it off. His property once included the road that headed straight to the ferry, so after years of people coming and going, it's not unlikely one or two would remain behind.

Vincent's daughter, Mary Winters, recalls once when she was sleeping in the house as a child, she woke to the sound of what appeared to be horses' hooves in the yard and people talking. She peered out the window just in time to see a carriage drawn by horses passing by. She described it as having a dark shape about it but clear enough that she could make out the carriage and the movement of the horses.

The Vincent property isn't the only one holding on to its past. Winter's grandmother once stayed overnight at the two-story house across the river (which is no longer there). In the middle of the night, she heard a chain rattling in the attic. When she looked outside her room and peered down the hallway, a lady in a long white dress walked by. And she wasn't alive. Her grandmother was so scared that she hurried back inside her room and refused to move for the night, Winters said.

CHAPTER 21
YOU SHALL NOT PASS!
HAUNTED BRIDGES AND ROADS

The haunted don't relegate themselves to buildings and homes. They roam the countryside, inhabit swamps and woodlands and sometimes plague those who attempt to pass on bridges.

More than one hundred years ago a man, carrying payroll, was robbed in the countryside outside the southwestern prairie town of Eunice. When the robber was caught, he was beheaded near the bridge over Bayou Des Cannes. Residents believe the robber haunts the bridge as a vision of a headless horseman crossing the bayou.

The "Headless Bridge" legend has been passed down through the generations, and many young people visit the bridge at night for the chance of seeing the lonesome body—or perhaps for other nefarious reasons. It's been routinely told that those who cross the bridge after dark suddenly experience car trouble and have difficulty starting their engines.

The tale has since gravitated to nearby Miller's Cemetery, now called "Headless Cemetery," where the unfortunate robber has been known to prowl.

"It was a gathering point when I was in high school," said Ilene Andrews, a native of Eunice. Ilene's an old friend, and I was prodding her for information on a 1997 ghost story I was doing for the Baton Rouge *Advocate*. "We used to go there in the middle of the night."

Today, the cemetery is patrolled, and those venturing inside late at night might be arrested.

So far off the beaten path that it's difficult to locate, near the German community of Robert's Cove, lies Hookman's Cemetery and Bridge. The small cemetery dates back to 1934, and some say the plots were dug for those who couldn't afford a better burial. Like the Eunice tale, a headless man haunts this area as well. Others reported seeing paranormal lights and experiencing strange electrical problems.

It's easy to surmise these two tales and cemetery-bridges have been birthed from the same legend.

The Paranormal & Spiritual Society Investigators (PASS) visited Hookman's Cemetery in 2008 and reported the following on their website:

"We were escorted by local area residents to the site. The graveyard was located on private property and ends in a circle driveway. The area around the fence has recently been cleared out. A short distance behind the cleared area the woods begin again. Visible from the fenced in area were locations that seem to be old tombs. They were made of old red bricks."

Their escort for the night had claimed to have heard a woman screaming one night when visiting the graveyard with friends. The incident happened after one of the girls stepped on a grave. She also recounted visiting the bridge and having their car suddenly die and become difficult to restart.

PASS didn't capture any paranormal activity that night, but they did hear unusual, unexplained noises in the woods by the bridge.

MR. HOOKMAN TO YOU!

Mary Alice Fontenot was a South Louisiana journalist and author of the beloved *Clovis Crawfish* children's book series. Born in Eunice, Fontenot wrote a historical column for the Crowley *Post-Signal*, including one concerning the "Legend of Hookman, Is it Real or Contrived."

Fontenot had heard the tales as well, but she pinpointed the cemetery in question to be Hanks Cemetery North, located between Crowley and Rayne, just north of the Rice Experiment Station on Caffey Road. (When I looked up Hanks Cemetery online, I found a reference to a cemetery located outside Morse, Louisiana, on Hank Cemetery Road between Crowley and Jennings. Perhaps the one Fontenot references is a separate cemetery, due to her mentioning it as being "north.")

To reach Hanks Cemetery North, Fontenot claims visitors should drive through the Rice Experiment Station a few miles north of Interstate 10, where the main road turns to gravel.

"A right turn at the woods leads to a small cemetery, which is neatly kept and surrounded by a hurricane fence," she wrote in the October 26, 1980 Crowley *Post-Signal*. "The graveled roadway, obviously constructed to give access to the burial grounds, is an ideal Lover's Lane. Yet it is said that teenagers are fearful of lingering in the vicinity. The spirit that haunts the place is not benign—it is a mean, vengeful ghost known as 'Mr. Hookman.'"

A hook has taken the place of the man's right hand, hence his name. He uses the sharp instrument to drag folks screaming from their cars when the autos have stalled at the graveyard. Some have even spotted the man crossing the road, Fontenot reported.

But the weirdest aspect of this tale involves a spectral bovine. If you walk three times around the giant oak tree at the edge of the cemetery, a ghost of a cow will appear.

Because people kept calling the Acadia Parish Library for information on the hauntings, library staff member Charlotte Stakes ventured out to the cemetery to see for herself.

"Charlotte walked around the giant oak three times," Fontenot wrote in her column. "She didn't even hear a ghostly 'Moo!' Under the tree was evidence that the place had been used for picnicking—empty cans, plastic spoons and forks were strewn about."

Perhaps she found an empty bottle of wine as well.

DON'T CRY "MARY"!

Just outside Lafayette in the suburb of Broussard is a lone stretch of highway called Bayou Tortue Road, which becomes Parish Road 140 once you leave the lights of the major Louisiana Highway 90 behind. It was along this winding road that a girl and her date, fresh from their prom, stopped at a bridge to hold hands and gaze into the waters below. But the girl's date, who had been drinking, had more than holding hands on his mind. When Mary refused his sexual advances, the date became violent, striking her with a whiskey bottle and dumping her body into the bayou below. The body was never found.

Locals claim to see a woman in white appearing on the Bayou Tortue Road Bridge at night, calling it "Mary Jane's Bridge."

Other tales regarding Mary Jane's Bridge are that of an ax murderer plaguing the countryside in the early 1900s.

One has to wonder who this Mary Jane is and how these legends arose without the discovery of a body. It's possible the legend of Mary Jane is just another teenage myth meant to scare other teens while driving in rural areas at night.

According to Tim Westcott in *Weird Louisiana*, if you travel to the bridge at midnight, turn off your car and utter, "Mary, Mary, Mary," the car will not start again until it's pushed off the bridge and out of the energy zone caused by the dead girl.

"Every year at midnight on the anniversary of her death, you can see Mary's ghost on the bridge," the author claims. "Dressed in a long white dress, she roams around the bayou where her life was tragically cut short."

TIME TRAVELING TO ABBEVILLE

Along the highway connecting Lafayette to Abbeville, a 1940s black sedan has been spotted with a woman in period dress at the wheel with a child next to her in the passenger seat. Sometimes, the woman motions to other cars for help but then soon vanishes.

Lafayette resident Ken Meaux heard the tale from a close friend who had a firsthand experience with the 1940s woman and child. He recounted it in his story, "Time Traveler," published in *Strange* magazine in the spring of 1988. Meaux's friend and traveling companion spotted the woman in the antique car on October 20, 1969, witnessed her distress and asked if she needed help, according to Meaux's account. The woman nodded, so the pair motioned to her to pull over.

"They saw her begin to pull over so they continued to pass her so as to safely pull over also in front of her," Meaux wrote. "As they came to a halt on the shoulder of the road, L.C. and Charlie [the fictitious names he gave his friends] turned to look at the old car behind them. However, to their astonishment, there was no sign of the car. Remember, this was on an open highway with no side roads nearby, no place to hide a car. It and its occupants had simply vanished."

CHARGING THE TEXANS

Arguably, the most haunted area near Lafayette is just outside the town of Sunset, named by railroad workers who finished the job at dusk where the town is now located, or so the story goes. Marland's Bridge, next to Chretien Point Plantation (see chapter 14) is the site of a Civil War battle known as the November 3, 1863 Battle of Bayou Bourbeaux between Union troops under the leadership of Brigadier General Stephen G. Burbridge and approaching Confederate troops led by Brigadier General Thomas Green. The Confederates took the Union forces by surprise, and chaos ensued, resulting in a solid victory for the South.

The hero of the day was twenty-three-year-old Lieutenant William Marland of the Second Massachusetts artillery. When Texans approached and appeared to be about to capture him, Marland charged the bridge across Bayou Bourbeaux. The surprise action forced the Texans to jump off the bridge into the water, and Marland escaped. He was later honored with the Congressional Medal of Honor for his brave actions that day.

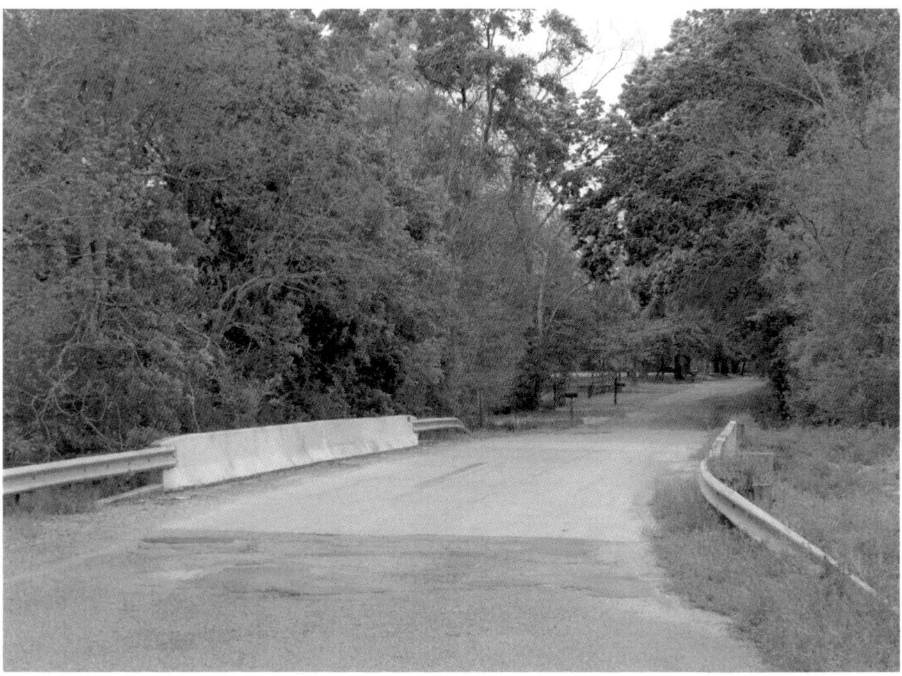

Civil War soldiers and a woman in white haunt Marland's Bridge near Sunset.

Today, the bridge is named for Marland, which might not be a good thing, for folks near and far claim the bridge and area surrounding the bayou as haunted. Locals have reported seeing unusual lights and hearing strange noises near the bridge, plus a woman wearing white has been spotted walking on the bridge—and she's anything but alive.

Louisiana Spirits made several visits to Marland's Bridge and recorded unusual phenomena and "a large orange light crossing the bridge." The photo is posted on their website.

Ghosts N Spectors Paranormal and Investigation and Research of Breaux Bridge experienced paranormal activity on three occasions at the bridge, including "phantom smells, disembodied voices, sub-zero temperature drops, unexplained free floating EMFs, shadow figures, feelings of being watched, feeling that you are being touched, and growls emanating from unknown origins," they reported on their website.

They claimed on the website report, along with a recording of the actual EVP, that:

> *One of our parked vehicles had the head lights and interior lights turned on when all investigators were across the bridge and this phenomena* [sic] *took place at the time we captured an EVP saying "get in your truck and leave." While walking the area on the anniversary of the battle, an investigator complained of sudden pain in the arm as if she'd been struck with something. After removing a jacket and rolling up a sleeve, a round red mark about the size of a dime was visible. The investigator reported feeling as if she'd been "hit" with something small and it burned like being stabbed with a hot iron. The description of the sensation is similar to that given by gunshot victims. The pain eased after about thirty minutes but the mark lasted a few hours then faded.*

CHAPTER 22

NOT SO FINAL RESTING PLACES

ACADIANA'S CEMETERIES

Loreauville is a quiet town nestled against the sleepy Bayou Teche. It is also the final resting place of King of Zydeco Clifton Chenier, buried in All Souls Cemetery. Some say Chenier still serenades Loreauville residents, but most just laugh it off as nonsense.

Mike Vital, Chenier's nephew and owner of the Clifton Chenier Club in Loreauville, once encountered a man who was sure the accordion he heard in the graveyard was that of the King of Zydeco. He recounted the tale in the June 27, 2010 issue of the *Daily Iberian* newspaper.

"This old guy would always walk in front of the club, and he happened to sneak up on me and told me he heard a guy playing accordion in the graveyard," Vital was quoted in the article. "Each time he would come, I would laugh and think he was old, senile or crazy. I'd go to the cemetery and look around and not see or hear anyone at all. He'd always come back when I was locking up and scare the hell out of me when he'd tap me on the back. I like to jump through the glass door. Eventually I said it had to be Cliff out there that he was hearing."

According to the article by Patrick Flanagan, the culprit was live zydeco musician Corey Ledet serenading Chenier in the graveyard.

THE LEGEND OF EVANGELINE

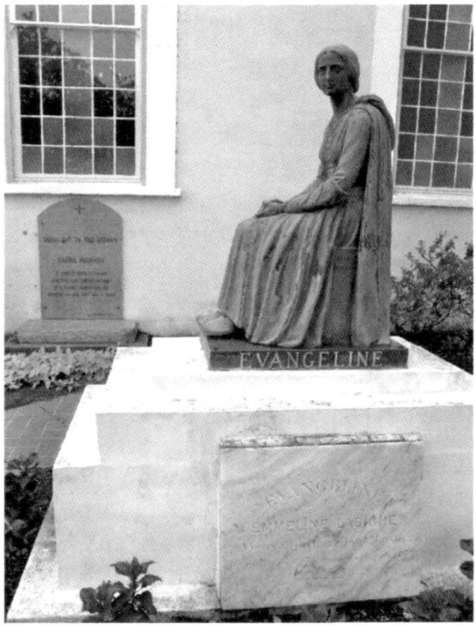

Emmeline LaBiche is said to have been the inspiration for Henry Wadsworth Longfellow's "Evangeline." Delores del Rio, who played Evangeline in the 1929 film, was the model for this statue placed on LaBiche's grave in St. Martinville.

Visitors to St. Martinville usually come looking for Cajun culture and history, even though the town was founded by French and Spanish colonists before *le grand dérangement*—or great expulsion—of the Acadians from the Canadian Maritimes that eventually brought the exiles into Louisiana. For in St. Martinville, a legend remains that dates back decades and is dear to the hearts of both Acadians of Canada and the Cajuns of South Louisiana.

When the Acadians were exiled from the Maritimes by the British beginning in 1755, they were scattered throughout the thirteen colonies, England, the Caribbean and, eventually, France. Some found refuge in Louisiana, then a Spanish colony that was glad to have Catholic citizens help settle the region. Upon arrival, the Spanish government awarded the Acadians land grants, equipment and seed to start a new life. The largest group—totaling 1,596 people—arrived between mid-May and mid-October 1785 in St. Martinville.

The Acadians settled within the region, including Lafayette, and later became known as "Cajuns." But for the most part, the world was ignorant of the massive expulsion from their homeland forced on this group, which resulted in almost half dying of exposure, disease and poverty.

In 1847, Henry Wadsworth Longfellow changed all that when he wrote the epic poem "Evangeline: A Tale of Acadie." The hexameter verse of an Acadian girl separated from her intended during *le grand dérangement* made the young poet famous. The poem follows the lives of Evangeline and Gabriel, two young lovers planning their wedding and life together in Grand Pré, Acadie, known by the occupying British as Nova Scotia. When the British forced the Acadians from their lands and exiled the peaceful residents to the American colonies and other far-off ports,

Evangeline and Gabriel are separated. Evangeline lands in Louisiana only to hear that Gabriel has arrived and left, looking for her. Evangeline then begins a lifelong search for Gabriel through the American frontier, eventually joining the Sisters of Mercy in Philadelphia until old age, when she finds Gabriel on his deathbed in a hospital. The two lovers have a moment together at last, but their reunion is tragically destroyed by Gabriel's death.

More than one hundred versions of the poem have been published, and two movies, both filmed in the 1920s, were made. The most famous film was the 1929 version starring Delores del Rio filmed in St. Martinville. A statue of Evangeline, created with del Rio as a model, exists on the grave of Emmeline LaBiche, a St. Martinville woman who Louisiana judge Felix Voorhies believed was the source of the story; he claims so in his *Acadian Reminiscences: The True Story of Evangeline* that he wrote in 1907. The gravesite and statue rest beside St. Martin de Tours Catholic Church, known as the "Mother Church of the Acadians."

Near the St. Martinville grave site is the "Evangeline Oak," where LaBiche waited patiently for her Gabriel, a man named Louis Arceneaux, until she went insane after finding out he married another. Louis Arceneaux's

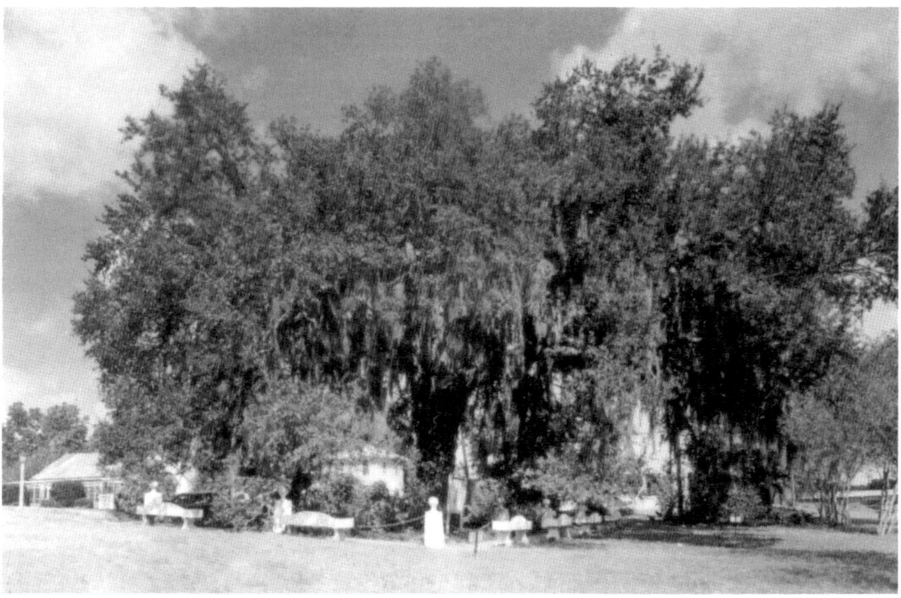

The Evangeline Oak, where Emmeline LaBiche waited for her "Gabriel," Louis Arceneaux, attracts tourists every year.

residence, titled BeauBassin after his Canadian Maritime home, is now on display as part of Lafayette's historical park, Vermilionville. At the original site of the home, however, the historical marker out front reads: "Here Louis Pierre Arceneaux, prototype of Longfellow's Gabriel, established his ranch in 1765."

Thousands of visitors come each year to St. Martinville to sit by the impressive oak tree where Emmeline waited so patiently for her beloved Louis Arceneaux and to gaze upon the face of Evangeline—Delores del Rio—in the graveyard at St. Martin de Tours.

GRAND COTEAU

There are ghostly rumors online about the historic Jesuit Spirituality Center of Saint Charles College in Grand Coteau, a peaceful spot where retreats are held throughout the year. Legends say that an old priest in Sunday vestments walks the grounds as well as various spirited nuns. The center fronts Martin Luther King Jr. Boulevard and the numerous boutiques and antique stores of the historic town, but a lovely church and cemetery exist at its back, the tombstones resting on a hillside overlooking pastureland and woods. I couldn't find anyone to verify the tales of the priests and nuns, but if I were to haunt a place, this peaceful oasis would fit the bill.

IN RAYNE THEY DO THINGS BACKWARD

B.L. Rayne brought the Louisiana Western Railroad to the prairie west of Lafayette, which gave the small town of Rayne its name. But it was frogs that brought it fame. The Weill brothers of France saw a future in the region's bullfrogs and began exporting them to restaurants throughout the country, earning the town the nickname as the "Frog Capital of the World."

It's hard to miss the connection. Across town, there are numerous frog murals created by award-winning Acadiana mural artist Robert Dafford and lots of various frog icons. In the fall is the annual Frog Festival.

One interesting feature of Rayne is the cemetery of St. Joseph's Catholic Church, where graves are buried in a north–south direction instead of the traditional east–west formation to greet the rising sun, a symbol of Christ's resurrection. No one knows for sure whether the grave organizers were having a joke on the town or if the mistake was unintentional, but St. Joseph's Cemetery is a rarity. In addition to frogs, Rayne is famous for its unusual cemetery mentioned in "Ripley's Believe It or Not!"

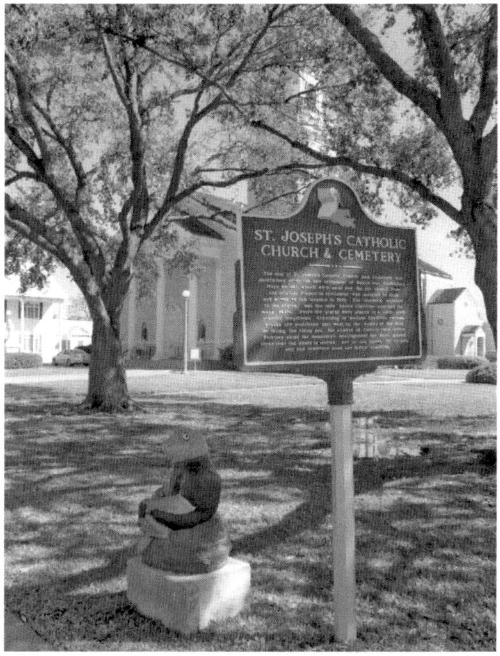

In Rayne, St. Joseph's Catholic Church includes a cemetery with graves buried in a north to south configuration, which is mentioned in "Ripley's Believe It or Not!"

An "Island" of Bones

Along the Louisiana coast, the wave action of the Gulf of Mexico has built up over time ridges of sand and shells. These "islands" appear above the horizon, dotted with live oak trees and named "chênièrs" by locals.

When Texan Jack Cole was herding his cattle through the prairies of southwest Louisiana, looking for better grazing land with a group of fellow cattlemen, he stumbled on one of these chênièrs, the tops of oaks and pecan trees waving in the breeze as if to entice him over. Cole was excited, wanting to venture farther, even though wetlands lay in between. His friends refused to follow through the murky swamp, so he set out alone, braving the bog and exploring the ridges beyond.

When he returned, he pulled pecans from his pockets to prove to his companions that he had made it to the "island." But his tales of bleached human bones lying on the ground from one end of the chênièr to the other made their hair stand on end.

Such is the story spun in *Louisiana: A Guide to the State*, written by members of the Writers' Program of the Work Projects Administration in 1941. The authors maintain that Cole settled on the island, despite the bones strewn about, but failed to solve its mystery. There are speculations, of course. One is that the Attakapas Indians, native to the region and thought to have been cannibals (although the claim has never been proven), took their prisoners to Pecan Island and left nothing but their bones after they enjoyed them as a meal. Another maintains that Privateer Jean Lafitte buried smallpox victims here, and the disease spread to the natives, who died en masse.

When the Smithsonian Institution arrived in 1928 to study the twenty-two large Indian mounds on Pecan Island, the human bones were nowhere to be found. The excavation did unearth lovely pottery, effigies and proof of a people living there long before the Attakapas. Unfortunately, treasure hunters looking for Lafitte's gold and coins or Native American artifacts have destroyed many of the mounds and, likewise, the region's historic integrity.

In 2005, another bandit arrived. Hurricane Rita tore up the region, flooding and destroying homes and uprooting coffins from cemeteries, which floated miles away. Rita turned the quiet rural area of live oak trees and pecan groves into a ghost town. Slowly, the residents rebuilt and returned.

Today, Pecan Island, with its nearby Rockefeller Wildlife Refuge and proximity to the coast, is a hunter and fisherman's paradise, plus a pristine location for birders. Look closely, however, if you're traipsing the chênièrs. There might be a ghost or two with the answers to the Pecan Island boneyard.

CHAPTER 23

WHAT'S HAUNTING THE SWAMPS AND BAYOUS?

The swamps of South Louisiana can be a cacophony of noises, from frogs singing to alligators bellowing and everything in between. Or they can be eerily silent with nothing but the sounds of your paddle plying the placid, muddy waters. Add the soft touch of Spanish moss on your head or the dropping into your canoe of one of the many resident snakes, and Louisiana's wetlands provide quite a scare.

It's one of the reasons horror film directors come to the Bayou State to shoot.

But there may be some substance to the legends and tales that come out of the swamps and bayous of South Louisiana. Take the unusual lights that appear in woods or swamplands at night. Cajuns call them feu-follet, small balls of light that hover over land and water. Are they evil, as some believe? Or perhaps they are the souls of unbaptised children destined to haunt the nighttime. Either way, you don't want to follow these phosphorescent lights.

"The feu-follet, sometimes called simply follet, is an evil spirit which pursues its victims and causes them to lose their way in marshy places or in the dark and winding bypaths of a forest," according to "Early Louisiana French Life and Folklore" of the anonymous Breaux Manuscript, one of the few early writings about Cajun life.

The young author was returning home one night when a light resembling a lantern burst forth from a "bramble patch." Entranced, the young man followed the light to the edge of a deep swamp. At the last minute, he managed to break free of its trance before it did him harm. He threw his hat into the

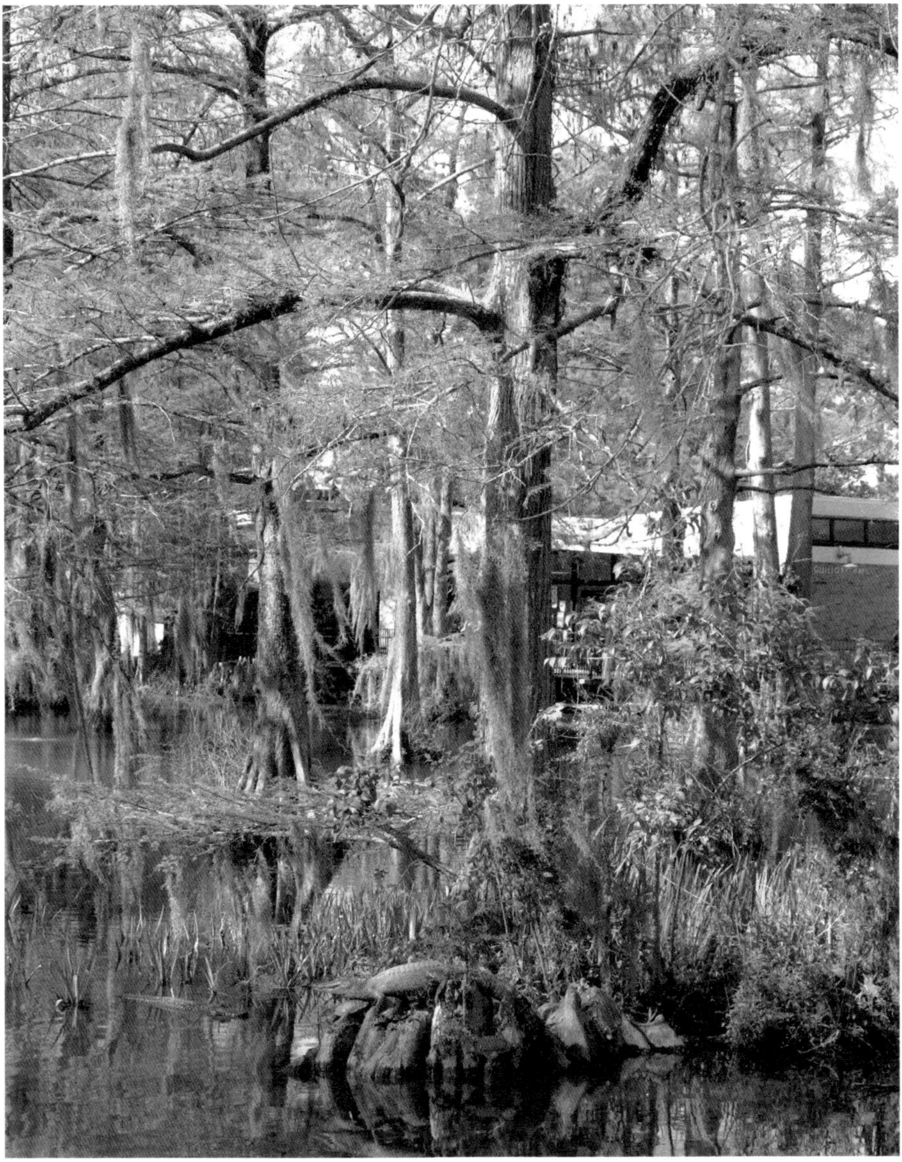

The University of Louisiana at Lafayette has a swamp at its center, complete with alligators.

water so the light would follow it instead and, while it was preoccupied, ran for home. The next day, the hat was found floating on the water.

"It [the feu-follet] was taken as an evil omen, and when seen approaching one's house, a knife had to be driven into the gatepost to keep harm from coming to the family within," wrote Damon Veach in "Acadiana's Eerie 'Feu Follet'" in the December 23, 1979 *Sunday Advocate* of Baton Rouge.

On the other side of the Atchafalaya Basin from Lafayette is the small town of Gross Tete, which literally means "Big Head" in French. Residents have seen a light floating at the hump of a deserted road and claim it's the ghost of a man beheaded by a moving train.

"As a child, I often recalled my grandmother and mother talking about these lights," writes Louisiana native and paranormal investigator Brad Duplechien in *Paranormal Uncensored*. "According to them, if you would see one of these strange lights, it was an omen that something bad was going to happen. When describing the lights, they simply said they looked like glowing balls of orange light, about the size of a volleyball, which could be seen literally bouncing across fields, most commonly near cemeteries."

Duplechien once spotted a strange ball of light crossing Highway 29 near Bunkie, about an hour north of Lafayette. At first, he thought the light to be an approaching motorcycle or car. But then, a car made the turn up ahead, and he witnessed the light for what it was: a feu-follet.

"The strange light then continued to literally float on to the other side of the road and faded into the overgrown weeds," he wrote, adding that he stopped and saw no signs of lights, fire or smoke.

"As I began to roll off, I looked to my right and there, to my surprise, was a small cemetery," he related.

Scientists claim these lights, also known as "will-o-the-wisps," are the result of gases being released from rotting vegetation. Since South Louisiana contains miles of nonmoving water sources, feu-follets would naturally thrive here.

"Numerous references in chemical texts refer to the light appearances as luminescence," wrote Veach. "Louisiana woodlands, marshes and swamps offer ideal settings for these almost instantaneous lights. Another term applied to this strange glow is directly related to a fermentation process, again part of nature's ability to break down particles into new forms."

But for some residents of South Louisiana, feu-follets are simply evil.

"*Et le monde avait une frayeur que si le fufollet aurait tombé sur eux, il les aurait tués*," is an expression recorded in the *Dictionary of Louisiana French*. In English, "And the people were terrified that if the will-o'-wisp landed on them, it would kill them."

LOUP GAROU GONNA GET YOU

Another favorite tale Cajuns love to share with their children is that of the loup garou, a Louisiana French werewolf, if you will. Cajuns describe these hairy creatures as shape-shifters, monsters that terrorize people and dance in the moonlight on St. John's Eve, June 23, at Bayou Goula.

"The loup-garou is a man-wolf that can walk upright on two legs, has large red eyes and a pointed nose, and appears to be a wolf in every other respect, including having shaggy hair and long, pointed nails," writes Christopher K. Coleman in *Dixie Spirits: True Tales of the Strange and Supernatural in the South.*

The *Dictionary of Louisiana French* defines it as a "werewolf, weredog, or other man-to-animal transformation of Louisiana folklore."

Cajun filmmaker Glen Pitre recalled a tale told to him by his *parrain*, or godfather, in *Swapping Stories: Folktales from Louisiana*. South Louisiana oyster fishermen were concerned when they found their oysters separated and culled, many of them eaten, with no evidence of it being done by humans. One day, a fellow ran into camp claiming he had seen a "creature that was huge and hairy and moved very quickly." The oyster eating ceased, but for the one who saw the creature, the nightmare just began. The creature haunted him, visiting him in his bed at night. He became so obsessed that people stopped listening to him, and his fiancée pulled out of the wedding. He grew to be an old man still seeing the creature, until one day he accidently cut the loup garou on his shoulder with the edge of an oyster shell, and it died. Ironically, the man lost the only friend he had.

Cathy Landry of Alexandria told me of the time she and a group of five ventured to the Mississippi River side of the levee near the Belle Chasse Research Center in Belle Chasse, outside New Orleans. This was the 1970s; they were young, and they had traveled to the levee to retrieve something from her brother's car. For some reason, the car was on the river side of the levee, lodged in the trees.

It was three in the morning, and the group stood on the levee top, shining flashlights into the trees in the hopes of locating the car. Naturally, they longed to retrieve the item and get out of there quickly.

And that's when the creature appeared.

"We saw two red glowing eyes, about a foot apart," Landry recalled.

At first, they thought it was a reflector on the car door.

"But then the two lights we thought were on the door starting standing up," she said. "It turned out to be about six feet, and it kept going."

The group hightailed it out of there, but not before hearing this "dark shadow" of a creature ripping the car door off.

In the morning they returned. Sure enough, the car's door had been peeled back like a banana.

"We all saw it," Landry insisted. "And a lot of other people have seen it out there."

Author Rita Monette calls it the "Rougarou," another name for the hairy beast, this time an all-white creature that roams, causing havoc until someone attacks him and draws blood. This allows the rougarou to turn back into a man. This old South Louisiana legend inspired her to write her young adult novel, *The Legend of Ghost Dog Island*, in which a ten-year-old hears howling coming from a nearby swamp island.

"This legend is said to usually happen within the smallest of towns in Louisiana, because of this the rougarou is often already known by its killer," Monette wrote on her book blog. "Before the dying man takes his last breath of life he will warn his savior that he cannot mention a word of the incident to anyone for one full year, or he too will suffer the same fate, and become the rougarou."

Monette recounted a story of a boy who was followed by a white dog, nipping at his heels. Frustrated, the boy slashed the dog with his knife. The animal then turned into a man, claiming he had sold his soul to the devil for money. He warned the boy not to speak of the incident, lest he suffer the same fate. Being a young kid, the boy told his friends. Immediately, he started disappearing at night until one day they found his body in the town's streets.

Unexplained creatures have been spotted across the nation, but when Matt Hoyle wrote the book *Encounters with the Strange and Unexplained*, he used the photo of "Denty" on the cover, a man who claims to have seen a swamp monster in the Honey Island Swamp near New Orleans.

"I was deep in the heart of the swamp on Honey Island when I saw the beast," Denty explained. "He was crossing a stream to the underbrush and at first I thought it was a bear, but when I got closer I saw the shape of it—more man than animal. I remember his eyes—amber and set far apart and his arms were really long. I didn't want to shoot and miss this one and I didn't think one bullet would do it so I got out of there as fast as I could. I'll never go to that place in the swamp ever again."

UNE GROSSE BÉTAILLE

If you hear a dog howling, someone you know is dying.
—Kaplan superstition

In the 1940s, there was a jaguarandi reported in Florida, a wild cat native to Central and South America and sometimes southern Texas. The animal sports short and rounded ears, short legs, an elongated body and a long tail.

When an article surfaced of the Florida cat sighting in the New Orleans *Times-Picayune* newspaper, Louise Veronica Olivier of Arnaudville contacted the paper to report her own unusual hairy animal—this one spotted along Bayou Bourbeaux in St. Landry Parish, just north of Lafayette. She called her creature "*une grosse bétaille*."

Reverend Jules O. Daigle in *A Dictionary of the Cajun Language* defines *bétaille* as "almost all unknown bugs or animals, also for humans to denote bestial qualities." *Dictionary of Louisiana French* has several definitions for the word, which include bug, worm, beast and monster. Naturally, a *gross bétaille* is an animal or bestial man of large proportions.

Olivier explained that Rameau Quebedeaux had spotted *une grosse bétaille* at midnight one night in June 1942, but no one believed him, chalking it up to "whiskey talk." Then Antoine Lanclos admitted to seeing a dog "with evil intent" while plowing his fields.

"He said he had called his own dog 'a la recousse,'" Olivier recounted in the *Times-Picayune* article. "In the interval between his dog and the encroacher, Antoine made good his escape."

Unfortunately, his dog was never seen again.

Someone in nearby Prairie Basse claimed a wolf was killing the resident dogs and "dragging them to the bayou banks." Chickens and turkeys were disappearing and cows and calves being spooked for no reason. As word spread, people avoided going out at night.

One evening, a group of residents were gathered together when they heard the distressing cries of dogs. They grabbed their guns and headed out.

"In the thicket of weeds and brambles was *la grosse bétaille* feasting on Ti Louie's Fido," Olivier recalled.

The animal was described as resembling a police dog with a large mouth and neck, heavy coat and a slender body that tapered to the rear. When approached that night, it let out a ferocious growl. The resident who plugged the creature later recounted the story to the parish priest.

"For while they might stretch the truth in ordinary conversation, none would have dreamed of speaking except in utter sobriety to *le bon Pere* who ministers to all their spiritual needs," Olivier concluded.

MADAME LONG FINGERS AND TATAILLES

Karlos Knott of Arnaudville makes excellent beer through his company, Bayou Teche Brewing. One day after a tour of his new facility, we got to talking about ghosts and legends. He was told as a child that if he didn't behave, Madame Grand Doigt would get him, arriving at night to eat his toes.

In English, Madame Grand Doigt means Mrs. Long Fingers, but Knott envisioned the woman with incredibly long fingernails capable of sliding said nails into door locks so she would have easy access to bad little children.

Mrs. Long Fingers has to be related to the *tataille* or Tai Tai, part of the larger boogeyman family. Blanche M. Lewis wrote in the *Attakapas Gazette* that the Tai Tai were giant bugs, "usually a roach," that came after bad children at night, which would definitely be enough to scare my roach-fearing sister after any wrongdoings. Roaches grow quite large in the South Louisiana swamps, and they fly.

The *Dictionary of Louisiana French* defines *tataille* as a "threatening beast or monster." The reference book further states that "ta-taille is said to be a giant creature that resembles a cockroach. It comes after dark and cuts off the toes of mean children."

"All my life, we heard that the Tai Tai (or however you spell it) was going to get us if we weren't good," said Lafayette resident Judy Bastien. "Also, when someone was looking really bad, like unkempt, you might say they look like un Tai-Tai."

"Tai Tai's were only supposed to scare little ones into not digging or wandering off," said Alice Guillotte of Lafayette. "'Stop or Tai Tai will get you.' Later, Tai Tai would be used as sort of joking about what might be out in the dark like a boggie man. A little bit serious."

DEMONS IN THE DARK

In all of Duplechien's paranormal investigating, the Fort DeRussy Cemetery in Marksville was his scariest experience. A friend of his recounted visiting the remote cemetery and hearing scratching on the side of his pickup and his girlfriend feeling like she was being choked. Another person riding in the back seat witnessed a "small black creature" about three to four feet tall attempting to crawl into his pickup.

Duplechien had heard of a "Devil's Run," a small black creature known to inhabit cemeteries and who prefers pregnant women (the back-seat rider was pregnant at the time), so he set out to investigate the cemetery himself. He made more than one trip to the eerie place, and each time felt dread and lost power of his equipment.

After reading of his exploits and spending a night in Marksville one summer, I ventured out to the cemetery with two companions, a fellow journalist and a local resident. My co–ghost hunters were in light spirits, but I immediately felt dread upon turning down the dark lane to the burial site, as if my asthma was kicking in. We parked just outside the gate, the headlights shining inside, and got out, my two companions laughing as if this were great fun.

Immediately, behind us we heard a noise that can only be described as a key turning an engine that is already engaged, like gears grinding. But the car we were driving had been turned off. I quickly shot some photos and begged my friends to retreat. They were still eager, despite the noise we all heard, but I wanted no more of the visit.

The next morning, I found a solid ball of light floating among the gravestones in one of my photos.

Feu-follet? Something more sinister? Or nothing at all? You be the judge.

Afterword

People continually ask me if I've had experiences since visiting haunted establishments in Lafayette and surrounding regions. Sadly, I've not—at least not the visual kind.

I suffer from asthma, which came on later in life due to my allergies. The only time my asthma hinders my life, however, is when I have a bad cold or flu or am suffering from hay fever in the middle of allergy season.

However, I've noticed my asthma kicking in when I visit haunted buildings. One can easily chalk it up to dust or mold allergies, but it's definitely been a pattern. For instance, the minute I entered the Opelousas Museum and Interpretive Center, my asthma symptoms began, gripping my chest like a vise and remaining that way until I left the building. I had the same reaction at the Grand Opera House of the South but only on the ground floor, which is routinely used for weddings and special occasions and kept spotlessly clean. Fort DeRussy Cemetery in Marksville kicked it in nicely as well.

I've also had those freaky feelings on occasions, ones when you know something is just not right. I've never felt frightened in any of the places I've visited for this book (well, maybe Fort DeRussy Cemetery in Marksville), but sometimes, the energy felt distorted. And I have always felt right at home at the quaint T-Frere's Bed and Breakfast in Lafayette (and recommend it as gracious accommodations), but a friend of mine felt an intense sadness on the second floor.

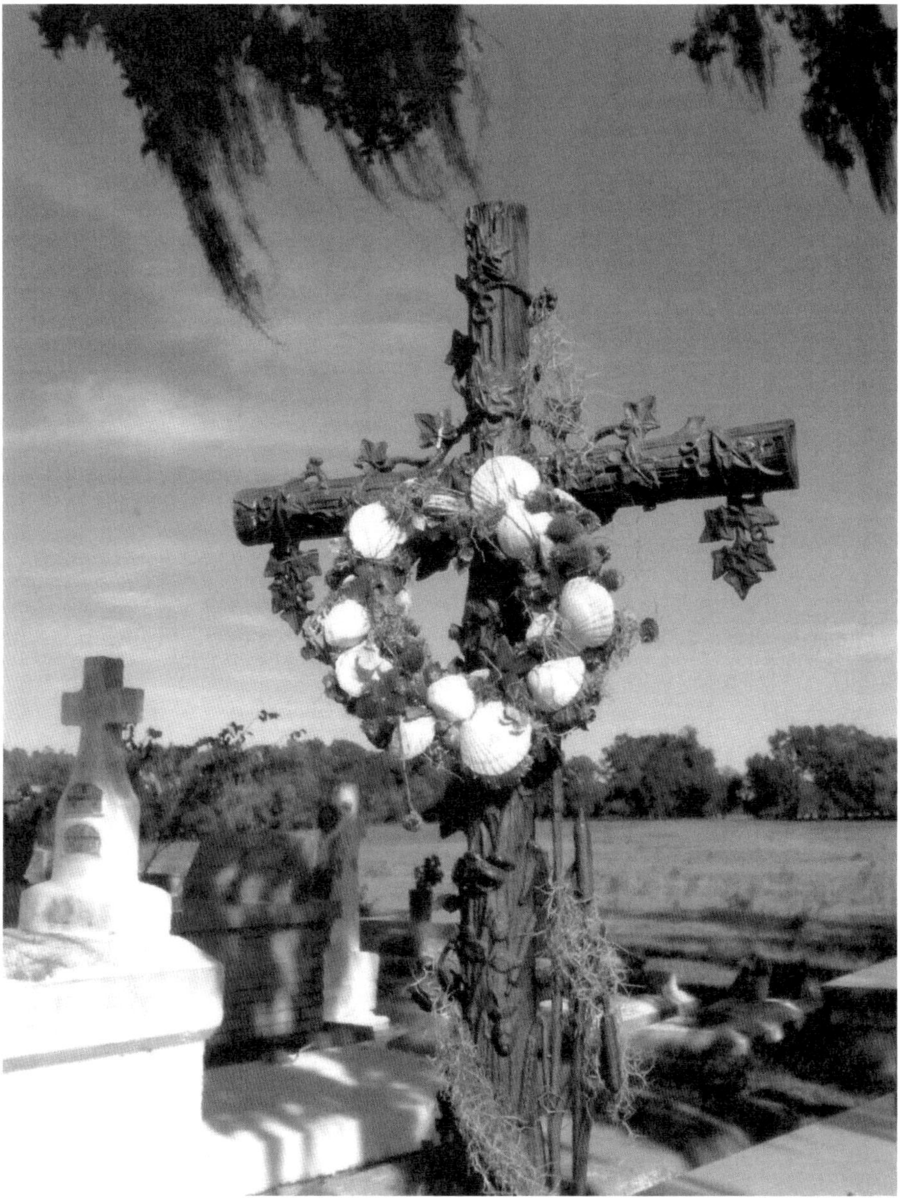

The peaceful cemetery at Grand Coteau.

Almost all the sites mentioned in this book are accessible and open to the public, so I hope you will find time to visit. If you have a ghost encounter, please let me know!

BIBLIOGRAPHY

Books

Arceneaux, William. *No Spark of Malice: The Murder of Martin Begnaud*. Baton Rouge: Louisiana State University Press, 1999.

Bradshaw, Jim, and P.C. Piazza. *Our Acadiana: A Pictorial History of South Louisiana*. Lafayette, LA: Thomson South, 1999.

Coleman, Christopher Kiernan. *Dixie Spirits: True Tales of the Strange and Supernatural in the South*. Nashville, TN: Cumberland House Publishing, 2002.

Daigle, Reverend Jules. *A Dictionary of the Cajun Language*. Ville Platte, LA: Swallow Publications, 1984.

Duplechien, Brad. *Paranormal Uncensored: A Raw Look at Louisiana Ghost Hunting*. New York: iUniverse, 2008.

Guilliot, O.C., "Dan." *Images de Lafayette: A Pictorial History*. Lafayette, LA: self-published, 1992.

Hebert, Donald J. *L'Eglise du Marais Bouleur: History of the Church at Marais Bouleur*. Mire, LA: Hebert Publications, 1991.

King, Gilbert. *The Execution of Willie Francis*. New York: Basic Civitas Books, 2008.

Lindahl, Carl, Maida Owens, and C. Renée Harvison. *Swapping Stories: Folktales from Louisiana*. Jackson: University of Mississippi Press in association with the Louisiana Division of the Arts, 1997.

Louisiana: A Guide to the State. New York: Hasting House, 1941.

Mamalakis, Mario. *If They Could Talk: Acadiana's Buildings and Their Biographies*. Lafayette, LA: Lafayette Centennial Commission, 1983.

Manly, Roger. *Weird Louisiana: Your Travel Guide to Louisiana's Local Legends and Best Kept Secrets*. New York: Sterling Publishing, 2010.

Perrin, William Henry. *Southwest Louisiana Biographical and Historical*. New Orleans, LA: Gulf Publishing, 1891.

Seebold, Herman Boehm de Bachellé. *Old Louisiana Plantation Homes and Family Trees*. New Orleans, LA: Pelican Publishing, 1971.

Stouff, Emile. *Chitimacha Notebook: Writings of Emile Stouff, a Chitimacha Chief*. Lafayette, LA: Lafayette Natural History Museum and Planetarium, 1986.

Valdman, Albert, and Kevin J. Rottet. *Dictionary of Louisiana French: As Spoken in Cajun, Creole, and American Indian Communities*. Jackson: University of Mississippi Press, 2010.

Voorhies, Judge Felix. *Acadian Reminiscences: The True Story of Evangeline*. New Orleans, LA: E.P. Rivas, 1907.

Word, Christine. *Ghosts Along the Bayou: Tales of Hauntings in Southwestern Louisiana*. Lafayette, LA: Acadiana Press, 1988.

Newspapers and Periodicals

Advocate, Baton Rouge, LA

Attakapas Gazette

Crowley Daily Signal, Crowley, LA

Daily Advertiser, Lafayette, LA

Great Scott Herald, Scott, LA

Independent, Lafayette, LA

Journal of Popular Culture

Times-Picayune, New Orleans, LA

Articles

Bernard, Shane. "J.D. Miller and Floyd Soileau: A Comparison of Two Small Town Recordmen of Acadiana." *Louisiana Living Traditions*. www.louisianafolklife.org.

Delcambre, Gerald J. "Post Office Preserves Colorful Bygone." *Morning Advocate (Baton Rouge, LA)*, September 17, 1967.

"Louis Michel Hanged: The Brutal Murder of the Robertsons Avenged at St. Martinville." *Times-Picayune (New Orleans, LA)*, March 25, 1983.
Manafi, Jessica. "Legends Say Acadiana, UL Host Restless Spirits." *Vermilion (Lafayette, LA)*, October 30, 2012.
McConnaughey, Janet. "Do Spirits Still Haunt the Bayou Darkness?" *Morning Advocate (Baton Rouge, LA)*, Dec. 31, 1985.
Meaux, Ken. "Time Traveler." *Strange 2* (Spring 1988). http://www.strangemag.com/highstrangenesstimetrav.html
Rohloff, Theresa. "Tourist & Culture Center Goes to City." *Great Scott (LA) Herald* 2, no. 2 (December 2005).
Veach, Damon. "Acadiana's Eerie 'Feu Follet.'" *Morning Advocate (Baton Rouge, LA)*, December 23, 1979.

Television Shows

Ghost Hunters. SyFy Channel.
Haunted Hotels. Travel Channel.

Websites

Aah T'Frere's House, http://www.tfreres.com
Bienvenue House, http://www.bienvenuehouse.com/
Café Vermilionville, http://www.cafev.com/
Chretien Point, http://www.chretienpoint.com/
Courtableau House Bed and Breakfast, http://www.courtableauhouse.com/
Ghost'N'Specters, http://www.ghostnspecters.info/
Ghosts of America, http://www.ghostsofamerica.com/7/Louisiana_Lafayette_ghost_sightings3.html
Grand Opera House of the South, http://www.thegrandoperahouse.org/
Louisiana Spirits, http://laspirits.com
Modern Music Center, http://www.musicalinstrumentstorecrowley.com/
Nash's Restaurant, http://www.nashsrestaurant.com/
Rice Theatre, http://www.crowley-la.com/DEPTrice.html

About the Author

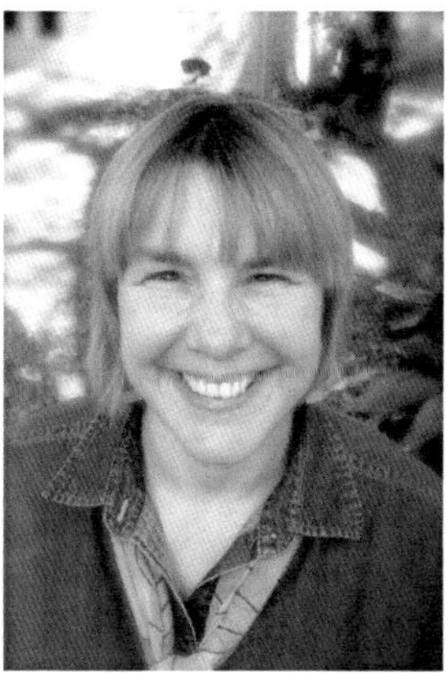

Cheré Dastugue Coen is an award-winning journalist and author living in Lafayette, Louisiana. A native of New Orleans, Cheré began her career in communications at the 1984 World's Fair. She has worked or written for *Variety* magazine in Hollywood, *TravelAge West* magazine, AAA, the *Advocate* newspaper in Baton Rouge, *Gambit Weekly* in New Orleans and the Gannett newspapers of Louisiana, among many other publications. She currently works as a freelance travel and food writer, plus pens the weekly books column and newsletter, "Louisiana Book News."

Her fiction includes the Kensington historical romances (under the pen name of Cherie Claire) *A Cajun Dream*, the *Snow Angels* anthology and *The Acadians*, a historical series of Emilie, Rose, Gabrielle and Delphine.

Her nonfiction books include *Exploring Cajun Country: A Tour of Historic Acadiana* by The History Press (2011), *Magic's in the Bag: Creating Spellbinding Gris Gris Bags and Sachets* with Jude Bradley (Llewellyn, 2010) and the cookbook travelogue *Cooking in Cajun Country* with Cajun Karl Breaux (Gibbs Smith Publishing, 2009). Follow her on Facebook, Twitter and her blog, HauntedLafayette.blogspot.com.